Street Corner Ching

The Ancient Chinese Oracle in Plain English

Randy Handley

Open Books PRESS

An imprint of Pen & Publish, Inc.
Bloomington, Indiana
(812) 837-9226
info@PenandPublish.com

www.PenandPublish.com

Copyright © 2010 The Street Corner Ching - Randy Handley

A Note to the Reader
Every effort has been made to ensure that the information contained in this book
is complete and accurate. However, neither the publisher nor the author is engaged in
rendering professional advice or services to the individual reader. Neither the author nor
the publisher shall be liable or responsible for any loss, injury, or damage allegedly arising
from any information in this book.

ISBN: 978-0-9842258-2-8

LCCN: 2009938848

This book is printed on acid free paper.

Printed in the USA

Contents

INTRODUCTION

When I was ten years old I rode my bicycle down to the library in Griffith, Indiana, walked up to the librarian and demanded a copy of *The Meaning of Life*, a book whose existence I had presumed, based on some vague discussions I had heard on the Sunday afternoon TV talk shows from Chicago. Local intellectuals would discuss heady matters with national intellectuals, in town promoting a new book perhaps, and drop little bombs of hope on my bewildered young mind in the form of phrases like 'the human spirit', 'freedom of expression' and 'the meaning of life'. As a kid from a blue collar working class neighborhood, this kind of talk was a revelation to me.

But the TV people never explained very much about their high-minded banter or told me what the meaning of life was, so I assumed it was something to be learned by reading a related book, and then moved beyond, as you would move on past the story of say, Sacagawea, after a history exam.

Such a book, I imagined, must be where the adults had put all the crucial information they were keeping from me. Most of them certainly acted as if they had it hidden somewhere.

The bemused Griffith librarian, in cool certainty that no such book was available, took this as an opportunity to show me the Dewey Decimal System, and then she was herself somewhat amazed to discover that the library actually did have a book on the shelf entitled *The Way of Life*, which was a translation of the *Tao Te Ching* of Lao Tzu.

She told me that I was too young for such a book but in my admittedly immature existential angst, I insisted that I must have it, and fairly ran off with the tome.

This was my perfect introduction to ancient Chinese philosophy and some of it was simple enough that I could grasp it right away, and all of it was beautifully powerful enough to move me in a way that mere comprehension does not touch. I still read it every year or so.

By the time I was out of high school and beginning to make a life for myself as a blues/rocker and singer/songwriter, I had heard of the *I Ching*, the ancient book of Chinese oracles, and had perused a copy once or twice.

In my twenties, after I was hired to write songs in LA, one of my first purchases as a nearly middle-class hipster of spiritual bent was a copy of the Wilhelm/Baynes translation of the *I Ching* which I then read over and over again, it was so fascinating to me.

I learned to throw the coins to make a hexagram, and set about to know my destiny. I was amazed at the subjective accuracy of the readings using the simple three coin method. But as the faint footnote of my musical career started down a path through disco disasters to a variety of stunning pop miscalculations, I sometimes became childishly, personally angry with the *I Ching*, even though I hardly ever really followed the advice or heeded the warnings I was given.

I put it down. I picked it back up and I looked at other translations. I decided it was not for me. I came running back in consternation.

At some point it occurred to me that the scholarly approach of all the translations I had seen was a little stilted and the language was often as abstruse as it was ancient.

I thought I should try to write a more accessible version of the book myself.

I asked the *I Ching* about it and received the first hexagram, with the sixth line moving. (What this means will be scribed presently, when I explain how to consult the *I Ching*.) The sixth line is a pretty nasty line about presumptuous arrogance.

I gave up the idea but decided to ask again in a year.

That was thirty-some years ago.

Every year I asked and every year I got a resounding "No Way", wrapped in various polite but pointedly negative imagery.

Since you have probably never heard of me before, you can well guess how my grand musical ambitions turned out, for the most part.

Actually, a lot of cool things happened for me in the music business. I wrote songs recorded by a bewildering variety of artists, from John Mellencamp and John Denver to Diana Ross and Garth Brooks. I got to play shows with personal heroes of mine like Dr. John, Townes Van Zandt and Etta James. I came achingly close to major label success as a recording artist on a few occasions and spent a lot of time riding around the country on tour buses, playing piano for guys like Lee Roy Parnell and in my own blues band. It's just that it all never amounted to "rich and famous", and sadly, "rich and famous" is usually the only real alternative to "broke and obscure", in today's show business.

So for the last ten years I have been doing what is called a Day Job or in my case, lots of day jobs, mostly in construction and home health care. I do, of course, still write songs and play music, but as I've gotten older, other interests, especially spiritual pursuits, have taken up more and more of my time. So I'm as likely on a given night to be poring over a spiritual essay, as I am to be looking for the local blues jam.

Along the way I studied several different spiritual traditions and learned from all of them. I became, and remain, a devotee of the great spiritual teacher Adi Da Samraj, but the *I Ching* was also never far from the center of my universe. After work, I spent a couple of years writing a spiritual memoir and had, by this time, come to assume that I was probably never going to get a green light from the *I Ching* on the project of creating an American interpretation of the text.

When I had finished the memoir and it was circulating among friends, I found that I had become addicted to being a writer, and so I decided to put my question to the Oracle one more time. In response I received the fifth line of the first hexagram, which is an auspicious and very encouraging reading: in some translations it indicates worthwhile spiritual achievement.

That was good enough for me.

Before I describe this translation and explain how to throw the coins, I will tell you one other story involving the reading of the Oracle. I must admit it is an odd one, but it speaks to the spiritual hodgepodge that is increasingly our heritage in the American melting pot, and it illustrates a point regarding how to approach the *I Ching*, so I include it here.

Many years ago before I became a fan of the *I Ching*, I was visiting Frank Fools Crow on the Pine Ridge Reservation, on the occasion of a powwow near Kyle, South Dakota. Fools Crow was a renowned medicine man, as were a number of his guests, and there was also a sizable 'New Age' contingent of mostly younger seekers who had come up for the weekend.

Catholics, Protestants, Buddhists, Yogis – all kinds of people were there, in addition to Fools Crow's many Lakota friends and relations. I was basically a young forager at the buffet of contemporary spiritual possibility and very much impressed with Lakota spiritual practices, as well as the lively variety of other views represented at this gathering.

One guy was demanding a lot of amused attention from the old timers around Grandpa Frank's little house. He kept asking questions of the various Wicasa Wiccan, or Medicine Men as they are more commonly called. Then he would run back to his van and throw three Chinese coins six times, doing a hasty, casual version of an *I Ching* reading, to see if the ancient Chinese oracle agreed with what he had just been told.

He was an anxious and rather rude young man who seemed to keep getting information that he could not abide.

I will never forget listening all night to the sound of coins bouncing against the metal floor of his vehicle, as he threw reading after reading, obsessively trying to either change or overcome the information he didn't really want to know.

He left early the next morning, and everybody laughed about it, including me, although I did not know then that I was destined to become that same kind of obsessive-compulsive geek on occasion, after I took up regular consultation of the oracle soon afterward.

His approach was an example of wrong-mindedness on a number of levels.

Why drive out into the middle of nowhere to consult a Lakota medicine man if you are then going to test him against an English translation of a five-thousand-year-old oriental spiritual authority? It's not like you're doing research for MIT; you just want to find out about your future.

Why reshape your concerns again and again when you have already got the definitive response to your question?

Maybe it's youthful error: you hope that if you can just rephrase your query in the right way, you will eventually get the answer you want.

You will not.

The truth is that we humans want our lives to work out wonderfully well, according to our preset plans and dreams, and we often blame the messenger if the news is contrary. This guy wanted so badly for things to go a certain way, that when he was told it wouldn't happen, he was no longer throwing an *I Ching* reading, he was throwing a tantrum with Chinese coins.

The good news about bad news, in the case of my reaction to the *I Ching*, is that after about thirty or forty years of frequently not getting what I wanted from it, I gained a couple of things.

1. I learned that I was often better off *not* getting what I desired, especially if I was forewarned of the situation.

2. Without realizing it, I had translated much of the wisdom and most of the essential fortune-telling aspects of the book into the speech and imagery of my own mind and culture.

It is important to note here that the *I Ching* is very much greater than a fortune telling oracle. In my opinion it is as great a source of traditional spiritual wisdom as any text known to man. The sublime version written by Deng Ming-Dao, The Living *I Ching*, to name only one, ranks among the loftiest spiritual poetry I have ever read. The earlier Legge and Wilhelm/Baynes translations are also marvelous.

One should not look to trivialize or oversimplify the *I Ching* any more than one would the Bible or the Gitas or the Koran.

On the other hand, there is an aspect of this work that is meant to provide simple answers, and to be practically helpful to everyone, without regard to class or spiritual predilection. Everyone seeks to discover where happiness can be found and how difficulties are to be overcome.

In fact, the realization that this oracle actually does work has produced, for some folks whom I personally witnessed, the first real inkling that any kind of spiritual reality even exists.

Another important bonus of consulting the *I Ching* is that, since it existed long before even the earliest literature of the mainstream religions of the modern world, it cannot be reasonably thought to stand in opposition to any of them.

Confucius is widely said to have written the *I Ching*, but "compiled" is really more like it, as he was also thought to have visited Lao Tzu, the founding figure of Taoism, to receive his instruction at some length, and in any case, consultation with some form of the Oracles predates both figures far into the mists of prehistory.

It is also said that Lao Tzu is supposed to have lived to between 160 and 200 years of age and a lot of the stories surrounding the legend of Confucius have the ring of apocrypha as well, but what is not in doubt is that a good many of the wisdom teachings of the *Tao Te Ching* and the *I Ching*, are the same.

So to engage the *I Ching* is to take a look into some of the most ancient wisdom of the human race. It is a glimpse, however, through the dark glass of many centuries of linguistic and cultural change, and what was in an ancient time the plain imagery of thought has become, in some instances, incomprehensible.

But the *I Ching* is systematic in its spiritual fluidity, and therefore it is possible to infer, from the whole of the system, and with the help of repetition and experience, what some of the more obscure readings may mean in any particular case.

You will not find it lacking either for philosophical depth or personal relevance.

Still the arcane language of earlier translations can be quite daunting, and there has been disagreement among scholars, even from the earliest recorded commentaries, about the real meaning of specific readings.

I speak no Chinese and am no historian, yet as I have continued to consult the *I Ching* using a wide variety of translations over the years, and life has presented its changes, more and more I have found myself saying: "Ah, *this* is what that reading really means, to me."

So this brief adaptation of *The Book of Changes* has a twofold purpose, based almost entirely on a lifetime of personal study, trial and error.

The first purpose is to reinterpret the oracular imagery in language that anyone on an ordinary American street corner could easily understand and readily use.

The second purpose is to bypass, for the most part, those more philosophical, numerological and obscure commentaries on the texts.

But the *I Ching* is not exactly a how-to manual either, so to dispense with the original imagery and flow of thought altogether would be both foolish and disrespectful. Sometimes an ancient reference to a particular scene, custom or even a number will evoke an intuition that only the questioner would really understand, and I have tried to leave that ability intact. Such are oracles.

I have simply tried to include the kinds of information I myself have found most useful, as if I were doing a reading for a friend.

I must also add a strong recommendation to anyone who is really serious about the *I Ching*, that they continue to study all the related literature, including the many, much more expansive translations or interpretations of the book itself. The Carl Jung introduction to the Wilhelm/Baynes translation, is by itself worth the price of that edition.

The fact is, however, that if you are having trouble deciding whether or not to buy a certain car or take a certain job, a detailed study of the Taoist or Confucian commentaries on the answer you have drawn may not add much to your understanding.

This humble offering is meant for ordinary, everyday consultation.

After many years of head scratching and rectification of multiple translations of the sometimes contradictory, ancient instruction, and more years of neurotic, even ridiculous complication of the *I Ching*, I have formed an opinion about what most of the lines may mean to a contemporary western reader, in response to an ordinary question.

Like any one of the thousands of *I Ching* readers on street corners all over China, I necessarily bring myself, my language, my personal experience and point of view to this work.

So this is one man's take on the Book of Changes, in ordinary language – no more, no less.

YIN/YANG
How To Consult the *I Ching*

You don't need to have a complex philosophical understanding of yin and yang to get an answer from the *I Ching*.

But some explanation of the idea is necessary, in order to have a more than superstitious grasp of what is going on here, because all the lines you will encounter are either yin or yang, or yin dynamically changing to yang, or vice versa. So before I describe how to throw the coins and obtain the *I Ching's* answer, let me talk a little philosophy.

Reality or the Tao, or God if you prefer, is One.

But everything in the universe is multiple, a part of a complex pattern, and everything that a human can experience has qualities that make it different from everything else.

The contrasting qualities and polarities of all things are the nature of yin and yang. They are pictured traditionally within a circle, which is the, Tao and separated by an S-shaped curve, with one side dark and the other light. The continuous curvature of the emblem means that they cannot be completely separated and they cannot exist without each other.

There is also a dot of dark on the light side and a dot of light on the dark side, and this indicates that nothing is completely one or the other, and brilliantly plants the seed of understanding upon which The Book of Changes is based. Light needs the contrast of dark to be seen, masculine and feminine require each other to exist – active and passive, hot and cold, hard and soft, the list goes on and on. In each of the examples just given, the former is a Yang quality and the latter, a Yin quality. And on it goes, ad infinitum.

Each of the sixty-four hexagrams of the *I Ching* is made up of six lines, and each line is either yin or yang, making 384 line oracles altogether.

Individual hexagrams and lines are regarded as yin or yang in their essential nature, but there is a subtle mixture of influences, depending on the situation.

A Yang line is an unbroken line:

A Yin line is broken:

This is an example of a hexagram:

Within the complex system of yin and yang possibilities, each of the sixty-four hexagrams has a specific oracle (text) and each line has a specific oracle.

The answer to your question will be either a hexagram by itself, or the hexagram plus specific lines within the hexagram, called *moving* lines because, not only is the hexagram an appropriate answer to your question, a moving line is also changing into its polar opposite, yielding yet another hexagram relevant to your question.

Based on how the coins fall, you will often receive more than one moving line in a reading, so that you will want to take into consideration:

- the first hexagram oracle,

- the moving line oracles, and

- the new hexagram, the one that is derived from changing the moving lines into their opposite.

Read together, they are your answer. Generally, moving lines will be the most specifically accurate answer to your question, and the rest of the reading will be more general.

Even the relatively simple process of throwing a three-coin reading is instructed very differently in different books, some oppositely, in fact, to others.

Do not be overly troubled by this, the key is consistency and sincerity.

Choose a method and stick to it, and let the intelligence of the Oracle sort things out.

❂

This Is How I Do It

Cup three same-sized coins in your two hands. Think about your question.

Shake the coins as long as you like and then let them drop on a tabletop or other flat surface.

If you get two tails and a head, that is an unbroken (solid), or yang line.

If you get two heads and a tail, that is a broken, or yin line.

If you get three heads, that is a *moving* unbroken line.

If you get three tails, that is a *moving* broken line.

Do the same thing five more times. Record each result on a piece of paper immediately, so you don't forget. Start at the bottom and draw each line above the previous one. Draw an unbroken line or a broken line. Put an x in the middle if it is a *moving* broken line. Put an o in the middle if it is a *moving* solid line.

When you have done this six times, that is your hexagram.

Look up the hexagram and read its Statement. How do you look it up? It's easy. You consult the Lookup Table on page 23; find the upper half of your hexagram on the top and the lower half on the left, and follow the column and row to where they meet: that's the number of your hexagram. Of course, you can always just draw your hexagram and thumb through the 'List of Hexagrams' in the table of contents until you find the one you have drawn.

If you have no moving lines, the Statement is your complete answer.

If you have moving lines, read the Statement and then look at the numbered lines corresponding to the moving lines you have drawn in the hexagram. (For example, if you marked the second line from the bottom as *moving*, read line 2.) The moving lines will have a particular bearing on your question.

Since moving lines turn into their polar opposite, you should next draw a new hexagram in which the non-moving lines stay the same, and the moving lines change, from broken to solid or from solid to broken. This new hexagram is also an aspect of your answer. Look it up and read its Statement (not its lines). Some say it is like a future card in Tarot, or what the situation is likely to turn into.

In some cases the new hexagram will be *the* answer to your question, in other cases the moving line or lines will seem more specifically important.

Always make your first question to the *I Ching*: "Are you receptive to my questioning right now?"

There is no point making a call if the line is busy.

If you insist on asking after you have been told that the Oracle is not receptive, your reading will be worthless.

What makes the *I Ching* work, as I contend it very definitely does? Is it a spirit, God, or synchronistic probability?

Completely define spirit, God, and synchronistic probability. That is the answer.

I am not being cute here. The answer does depend on your definition of terms. Personally, I see the *I Ching* as a master personality, a spirit, an irascible, hilarious and nearly all-knowing witness of human doings who cares about you spiritually and generally could not give a damn how this or that worldly matter is going to work out for you, except that spiritual compassion and some ancient, kindly etiquette have made it the project of this spirit to help you out, if you are sincere and respectful..

If all this sounds complicated, imagine trying to verbalize the act of riding a bike to someone who has never seen one before. It is better just to get on the thing and start pedaling, then it gets simple pretty quickly and soon it becomes second nature.

Keep in mind, though, that knowing how to ride a bike doesn't make you Lance Armstrong. People have spent lifetimes contemplating and perfecting their approach to this work.

☯

What About Contradictory Lines in a Reading?

The Book of Changes is all about the fluidity of possibilities. If you believed the future to be altogether set in stone, there would be little point in consulting the oracle at all.

So, apparently-contradictory indications really mean that an outcome is not yet inevitable.

How you and others respond to the situation is still in play, and different, even opposing, outcomes are sometimes yet possible.

In fact there are, more often than not, a lot of things that could happen in a given situation, and the blessing of the *I Ching* is most often the indication of what kind of conduct will most likely bring the good fortune you desire, or help you avoid a problem that might otherwise trip you up.

You are sometimes going to get oracles that you don't like and indications about your character that you would rather not hear.

That is part of spiritual growth, and the *I Ching* is ultimately, for all its practical usefulness, a spiritual guide.

☯

Miscellaneous Pointers

1. I am a fan of asking questions in the form of:"What will be the likely outcome of this action or situation?"Yes or no questions do not work well, generally, and only one possibility should be addressed at a time, because even when more than one possibility is mentioned in an answer, they are possibilities related to only one situation or course of action.

2. The *I Ching* is traditionally quite formal. Even in my street corner interpretation it is somewhat so, and it is not a friend or peer to be argued with. To assume too much familiarity, no matter how long you have been doing readings, is a disrespectful invitation to a confusing reading.

3. If you are comfortable praying or meditating before asking your question and lighting a candle or some incense to further set the time apart as a special, spiritual ritual or exercise, that is a fine idea.

4. You need not ask a specific question, and you may find out something more important to you, if you don't confine your reading to any preconceptions at all.

Hexagram Lookup Table

Find the upper half of your hexagram on the top and the lower half on the left, and follow the column and row to where they meet: that's the number of your hexagram.

Upper / Lower	☰	☳	☵	☴	☷	☲	☶	☱
☰	1	34	5	26	11	9	14	43
☳	25	51	3	27	24	42	21	17
☵	6	40	29	4	7	59	64	47
☶	33	62	39	52	15	53	56	31
☷	12	16	8	23	2	20	35	45
☴	44	32	48	18	46	57	50	28
☲	13	55	63	22	36	37	30	49
☱	10	54	60	41	19	61	38	58

Hexagram 1
Heaven (Creative)

The Statement

All Yang lines. The Dragon. The Big Bang. Thunder and lightning. Masculine.

This means great potential for action or creativity. By itself it is a positive and advantageous omen. But bear in mind that so much pure potential can carry a danger with it; it could become too much of a good thing.

The Lines

1 Action is not right in this particular case. The temptation is certainly there, but things are not in place. The image is that of a hidden dragon.

2 Others may have done well already by taking the action you envision, but in this case you will do well to seek out someone of experience and listen closely to them, before you proceed.

A dragon in a field.

3 You are already engaged in your action, so now you need to be hardworking and alert, even if you have to lose a little sleep to keep things on track.

4 Here you may want to make a leap of faith, and it could be a success.

But are you strong and centered, like Clint Eastwood's Dirty Harry character, or are you making a grab out of fear and desperation?

This will tell you how lucky you should feel. A dragon about to fly.

5 Your action promises success here, but since good counsel is probably close by, why not check in briefly, then act all the more surely. A good spiritual outcome. A dragon in flight.

6 The bigger they come, the harder they fall. Beware that your confidence could have become arrogance. Fate always turns on a bully or a braggart, in time. Even a dragon with great powers and abilities can go too far, and then fall even further.

(I have never seen a reading with all moving yang lines, or talked with anyone who has, but it is certainly a possibility. I would take it to mean potential so great that it can instantly turn into its opposing counterpart when required. A masterful dragon indeed.

In terms of probability, getting this reading is like having a coin land on its edge.

Its meaning is presumably very powerful, but what that meaning is would depend completely on the question.)

Hexagram 2
Earth (Receptive)

The Statement

All yin lines. Peace. Rain. Patience.

Since all the lines are yin, polar opposite of the previous Hexagram, you might think that it would mean inaction or an absence of potential.

But this is not true; a better understanding is *responsiveness*. After all, where on earth is there anything completely inactive or without potential?

The traditional symbol is a mare, who, far from inactive, nevertheless finds a passive response to the right stallion and the world goes on, new life is born.

The Hexagram by itself is a sign of good fortune and tranquility, if you are going in the right direction and responsive to experienced guidance.

The Lines

1 The direction here is not good. You walk on frost and should beware that ice is coming soon. The slippery slope, the tough sledding is to be avoided.

2 Your direction is right and your stride is strong. This is a slam dunk, not to show off, but because it is the best possible spontaneous move, a thing of beauty that also wins.

3 This line indicates the wisdom of a kind of inaction. Knowing when not to take credit or show your cards. The game is either not played out yet, or it is just not your game. In any case, you will serve no one by being showy here.

4 The game is over and you have neither won nor lost. No congratulations, no cause for blame. It's a push, a wash, basically, a non-event.

5 When the hero is himself a little stunned and overwhelmed by his achievement, the world falls in love with such humility. There is much good fortune here.

6 Responsiveness is not achieved, instead there is misunderstanding, possibly even a collapse into violence. Back off, big time.

(The meaning of all yin lines moving may be similar to that of all yang moving from Hexagram 1, with an added caution to be exceedingly careful. It is another extreme rarity.)

Hexagram 3
Seedlings

The Statement

Things begin to grow all around, a possibility of abundance begins to show up.

Maybe a neighbor will share his tools with you.

The Lines

1 Once you have found the right spot, it is not too soon to think about who might help you plant and harvest your crop. And consider as many critical factors as you can think of, as you begin your project.

2 Still, without enough rain and sun, there is not much to do yet, but wait.

Help and encouragement give some comfort, but it could be a long time before the harvest.

3 You could go hunting, but if you have no guide and do not know the area, the game will likely escape before you, and you will still be hungry. Stop.

Conserve for now and keep an eye out for a guide.

4 Someone may show up with a tractor and a plow, intimate knowledge of the land, and plenty of experience. The farmer might even have a daughter. What a stroke of luck that would be. Good fortune.

5 Sprouts are a beautiful, lush, green sign, and you may pick around the garden to come up with enough for a nice small meal now, but you are far from a Thanksgiving dinner, as yet. Small fortune.

6 Sometimes there is bad luck or bad timing, even after a good start. You may ride up on your borrowed tractor only to find that the farmer's daughter has run off during the same stormy night that washed your crops away. This is a sign of some bad blues.

Hexagram 4
Youth is Wasted on the Young

The Statement

Here is one of the few times that the *I Ching* speaks directly about consulting the *I Ching*.

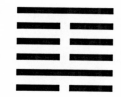

After all, the oracle did not come to you and ask for your help, you came to it and so you need to be respectful.

It says to ask your question once, sincerely, and not to continue asking about the same thing, whether you like the answer or not.

This is not an idle warning. You could drive yourself crazy or fool yourself into misguided, even disastrous actions, by ignoring this simple instruction.

In thirty-five years, I have made the mistake often enough to know, and even though the hexagram is usually translated Youthful Folly, it may be worth pointing out that we are all quite young compared to the Changes.

In youth, be determined. There is gain there.

The Lines

1 Punishment and discipline have their place in instructing the young and naive, but don't overdo it.

2 This is a good time to take a wife (or husband), at least as far as the happiness of having children is concerned. Partnerships are favored, generally.

3 Someone who would marry for money or sex alone, will be nothing but trouble to you in the long run. Avoid the greedy and superficial.

4 If you are inexperienced and distressed, and you ignore the wisdom that is offered to you, things will go badly. Wise up.

5 On the other hand, fate may laughingly reward some young innocent when he drops a dollar on the lottery, just to show the bitter old cynics a lesson. Good fortune for the innocent.

6 People used to say "Spare the rod and spoil the child." But harsh punishment is a lazy and ineffective method for teaching wisdom. In any case, the young or inexperienced are not to be treated badly, whatever their mistakes.

Who looks worse, the screaming mom at the K-Mart, or her unruly little brood of rug rats?

Be a good, reserved, compassionate example here.

Hexagram 5
Waiting

The Statement

Chill out, for now. Have a sandwich or something.

Confidence and timing are the keys to the future.

Waiting may sometimes seem harder than swimming a big river, but if you learn waiting, perhaps you can do both.

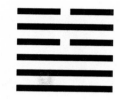

The Lines

1 You are fine. What is so wrong with the place you are in?

Don't borrow trouble. Don't be a drama queen. Just wait.

2 Okay, maybe this waiting is not ideal. Maybe you would like to take action or at least confront, say, a gossip.

Still, you show your power in waiting for now. A little talk is alright, too.

Good things will happen in time.

3 Waiting in the wrong place or for the wrong reasons may attract trouble. Be careful: if you cannot move stealthily away, stay wary.

4 Waiting that has turned into paralysis, in a dangerous place, leads to critical, very serious problems.

Flee, right now. Flood waters are rising.

5 This moment is like a picnic in good weather. You are chilling with friends here, enjoy. This is the essence of classy, confident waiting.

6 It is sometimes uncomfortable to be waiting around in a strange place and find yourself in the company of uninvited strangers (perhaps three strangers).

Be very patient and cordial. This was meant to be, and it will lead to good fortune.

Hexagram 6
Conflict

The Statement

In conflict, confidence is the key to facing your opponent.

A good first move is helpful, too.

Skill can do a lot, but nobody lasts forever.

Krishna told Arjuna to remember "me" and fight.

You could as easily say remember God or remember the Tao, when in conflict.

But conflict, even when inevitable, is not the way.

The Lines

1 Don't let things drag on and on. Let people talk trash all they want.

You will be fine at the end of this.

2 You can't win this time. Go back where you are comfortable and have some support.

Do not blunder ahead out of anger, pride or self-righteousness.

3 Maybe someone is taking care of you because of your good old days together.

How long can it last? In the end, your own good fortune should arrive.

But if you are playing second fiddle, don't imagine the applause is for you.

4 You win some, you lose some, and this conflict will not be won by you.

Reconsider things and make your own choices. Lose the battle, to win the war.

Understanding this, you will have peace of mind.

5 You can prevail here. You feel right and true, as winners do.

6 Too much conflict, or too much aggressive-mindedness, is like the boxer who doesn't know when to hang it up.

He may have the champion's belt this morning, only to have it taken away in the next round.

If he insists on yet another rematch, he will lose his dignity, too.

Hexagram 7
The Military

The Statement

The military requires three fundamentals: strong leadership, strong discipline and a strong code of honor. With these, things turn out well.

Soldier on.

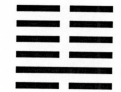

The Lines

1 Be sure the rules are followed and discipline closely monitored. One slip can sink a ship, as they used to say during World War II.

2 The center of a large force that is winning may be the safest place on earth.

You can expect promotion and perhaps a stroke of unexpected personal luck, as well.

3 There is no victory for the casualties. This line is a sign of defeat.

4 Even in war there must be rest. Even at rest there must be vigilance.

Find a good place to rest and regroup. It may be in the east.

5 You can capture what is needed now, provided the leader is not some green rookie, fresh out of boot camp. An inexperienced fool can only put you in harm's way.

You need a wartime consigliore, a battle-tested chief, to ensure victory.

6 A great leader appears and brings about a new order. He demotes the slackers, and gives extra rations and other rewards to his good men.

Hexagram 8
Come Together

The Statement

Coming together leads to good fortune.

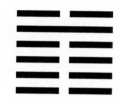

A further divination by a professional using yarrow sticks, will better illuminate your question, according to tradition.

Those who are unsure will likely come together soon.

But timing is everything in everything, and those who are too late will suffer.

The Lines

1 Again confidence is a key. To join with others is the way.

Trust this and another will come and share your good fortune.

2 You have friends or family who are already with you in spirit.

This is good.

3 The world is full of crooks and swindlers and sketchy characters. It is always best to avoid them, because even some fleeting, minor gain through questionable means, will diminish you in the end.

If such a brush cannot be avoided, get in, get on with it, and then get out as fast as you can.

4 When the value of cooperation is seen even by those outside your circle, this is quite fortunate, and leads to broader influence for you.

5 No one needs to be forced to join an enterprise that seems well organized and right; they will come along on their own. A wise leader steps up. There is gain and success on a large scale.

6 Without leadership, without intelligence and a moral center, the desire to band together brings misfortune. A mob may move forward, but only to chaos.

Hexagram 9
It's the Little Things

The Statement

The little things add up, like a barely visible, distant cloud eventually becomes the water in your glass.

It is not raining yet, though, so stay steady as a farmer, and just keep on keeping on.

Hot and sweaty as it is putting up the hay today, the cows will later give him all the nourishment he needs.

The Lines

1 Forget your question for a second. Remember what you would most naturally do, what it is your place to do, in this situation. Before the doubt of the question arose, you knew.

That is the right way now.

2 Circumstances, or perhaps a friend, will remind you of the best thing to do in this situation, but you may have to back off from your present position to see it.

3 Something has gone wrong, like car trouble or a mistake with money.

You may quarrel about it. Try to keep the quarrel as small as the trouble ultimately is.

4 Panic blows over, and you keep your cool. Good.

5 You are confident in your goal. Show that to someone close by, who has wealth to share or some way of mutually working toward it. You will not regret such an alliance.

6 Your cloudburst finally arrives, everything is in place and times are good. Everyone is relieved and doing fine.

Now have the wisdom to leave well enough alone.

Hexagram 10
Tread Carefully

The Statement

You have seen a man walk a tightrope. You have probably seen a firewalker, too.

You tread on a tigers tail; it does not bite.

You may go on.

The Lines

1 Stepping solemnly ahead is not a mistake, being aware of the dangers.

2 On the road less traveled, tranquil and straight, a hidden master strides in harmony.

3 Blind in one eye, lame on one leg, fools rush in, and the tiger bites.

Definite misfortune..

4 Be afraid, you have stepped on a tiger's tail.

But a tiger is also a cat, and may playfully roll its tail away; an apparently unlikely but fortunate ending.

5 If you must go forward now, then go decisively, although this is a situation where the outcome is not exactly clear.

6 Professional athletes spend hundreds of hours watching films of each other running.

How does the opponent go left, how does he go right, how does he turn on a dime, then shift and slide? They study to find his strengths, to emulate them, or to find a weakness in his game so they can exploit it.

In this case, study yourself as an opponent.

Learn these things about how you yourself tread and turn toward great fortune.

It won't be easy, but it is possible.

Hexagram 11
Prosperity

The Statement

Evil has gone, good has come, good fortune.

The high and mighty help those below, and there is plenty for all.

Continue.

The Lines

1 You may reach for something small and snatch up more than you thought.

Good fortune.

2 Go where you wish and take what you need. There is plenty to explore.

But don't go so far that you cannot hear a cry for help from your own friends.

Honor and moderation should balance exhilaration and acquisition.

3 There are always going to be setbacks, it is unavoidable.

Don't let that make you doubt your companions.

Get together for dinner and work things through.

4 Sometimes you seem to be just spinning your wheels, and no one else seems to be pushing.

This is not the time to lose faith in those around you.

5 A very meaningful and treasured gift may be coming.

Perhaps also a marriage.

This is a sign of a wonderful blessing.

6 An earthquake can happen even on a beautiful day, leaving everyone traumatized and in an exposed position.

Get organized and get help, but do not seek to make war on misfortune or anything else. You will only be shouting orders to an empty battlefield.

Hexagram 12
Clogged

The Statement

Wrong minded, wrong hearted people are holding things up.

No gain.

Even a master is blocked. He avoids false glory or comfort.

Good has gone. Evil has come.

The Lines

1 Amazingly, this first line is about the same as the first line of the last hexagram, despite the overall opposition in the situations.

Snatch your good fortune, quickly.

2 Flattery and subterfuge rule.

Great people cannot seem to get through.

Still, it appears to be your duty to keep trying.

3 There is shame here.

Whose is it? If someone uses their position to humiliate others, the shame is really theirs.

If you have done something to be ashamed of, listen to your conscience now.

4 Even in times like these, the solid commander or the valuable worker can gain some benefit with quiet perseverance.

5 Like everything else, a clog can only last so long, and it breaks down.

But the early flow of good fortune here could easily be lost without vigorous action to clear things up, and tie up loose ends.

6 Finally a flood of good washes away the evil and misfortune.

This, like the departure of a cruel tyrant, makes everyone glad again.

Hexagram 13
Society

The Statement

Families and nations are made of persons bound together by affection, not defined by their possessions or borders alone.

Moses led his people through the desert by faith and wisdom and to this day, that culture endures.

This is one example of the meaning of society.

The Lines

1 A street corner handshake and a simple conversation between friends can be the beginning of kinship, from which all the accomplishments of society eventually flow.

2 People may be brought together by mourning and remorse, as well.

A clan or even a street gang, are surely bound by their association, but in this case it is not a happy meeting.

3 Secret alliances against others, or perhaps someone else's attempts to ambush you, will not have success. Not a good time for action.

4 The inability to conquer a presumed enemy can be a blessing in disguise.

History shows societies blossoming after failing to conquer others.

After catastrophic attempts at conquest, the phenomenal revitalization of Germany and Japan after WW II are two modern examples.

5 The best struggle is the one that is settled before it takes place.

A show of force may be called for.

Great armies wail and prepare for the worst, but later meet and laugh with relief.

6 All societies value sacrifice of some kind. Service, fasting, prayer, communion, offerings of incense, song or food are common.

The purpose is transcendence of self concern for the greater good.

Here a ceremony in the open, maybe in the countryside, like the baptism of Jesus in a river, sets aside all regrets, and shows the value of society.

In any case, you can be open about your sincere relationships now.

Hexagram 14
Plenty

The Statement

The time favors you in a big way. General wellbeing and even wealth are possible.

Be noble, humble and generous. Work to deserve it.

The Lines

1 Being above jealous slander, you avert disaster.

You can weather difficulty if you are without fault.

2 Plenty sometimes requires plenty of action.

Load your pickup and set off to market.

3 When you are in a position to make a great offering, what a blessing it is to do so.

It is also wise to do so.

4 If you are gifted, who gave you your gifts? If you are strong, who gave you your strength? He who has more also has more duties and responsibilities, as a matter of course.

5 Plenty in the case of one who is also noble can even become majestic. If people feel your genuine love and respect, your actions will be seen as regal.

6 Divine blessing cannot be opposed. Supreme fortune.

Authentic, heartfelt spirituality is the greatest gift, and magnetically draws all good things to you.

Hexagram 15
The Humble

The Statement

It is wisdom to be humble. In a person of more elevated social circumstances, we call it nobility.

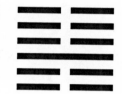

A noble person can balance and adapt, taking from what has grown too large, nourishing that which is too small, and getting good results all around.

In American culture showing any humility is often considered a disingenuous public relations move, or a sign of weakness. Still, it is better to be humble and have people misunderstand you, than to join the foolish, bombastic crowd.

The Lines

1 A humble person can accomplish even something difficult and get surprisingly good results.

2 As a great singer is immersed in the song, the truly modest can engage and complete whatever they have to do, without a thought of themselves. Success without complications.

3 When you roll up your sleeves and get a good sweat going, even if you could have let somebody else do the heavy lifting, this gets the job done, and promises a good outcome.

4 There is an easy and natural humility in this situation; rewards easily and naturally follow.

5 Do not allow yourself to be eclipsed by being too humble. This is a trick the unscrupulous might try to use against you or an illusion caused by ignorance in those who should know better.

You can be forceful if that is what is called for, without losing your integrity or your good fortune.

6 False modesty will shrink in a time that calls for decisive action; true modesty acts but does not let things get out of hand.

This is not the time to hide your light, or let anyone else shade it either. Success.

Hexagram 16
Excitement

The Statement

Elsewhere called delight or enthusiasm, here we have a situation where a happy period allows for the forward movement of our desires, and union with our friends and allies.

It is somewhat like the feeling after a huge thunderclap unexpectedly startles everyone and then we laugh because we know that no harm has been done.

Ceremonial worship can be exciting, too, as anyone who has attended a Holy Ghost gospel service or listened to a stirring and complex raga can easily attest.

A certain amount of excitement is simply a natural human response to those times when conditions are good enough to allow us to express our passion and spirit.

Even when he is startled, the sincere worshiper does not drop his offering.

The Lines

1 There's one in every crowd, of course, the pushy thug who has to make a scene out of a simple celebration.

Don't be this guy. Misfortune.

2 Being solid as a rock and straight as an arrow, you can see results ahead of time, and before the day is out, good things happen.

3 Wide-eyed excitement is usually over the top and self-indulgent. It can even become quite hazardous, if it distracts you from the right time for action, and you miss an important opportunity.

4 Maybe you are, yourself, the star of this line, the source of all the delighted excitement. People gather around you and nobody doubts your endeavor.

5 It's hard to get excited about anything when you are sick. This line indicates a chronic problem, which is not fatal, but which certainly undermines even simple enjoyment.

6 Many exciting things can turn to darkness, if you become devoted to the illusion of excitement for its own sake.

How thrilling it must have been in 1937, to stand with fifty thousand others cheering Hitler on, before all the death and devastation came.

How seemingly profound the rush of the addict's first taste of heroin. This is dark excitement.

But it can be turned around, even if it has taken a long time to see it clearly.

Hexagram 17
Following

The Statement

To follow is also to serve. If you follow and serve whatever is good and pure, you will have nothing to regret, and sleep like a baby at the end of the day.

The Lines

1 Something has changed in the power structure which could be to your advantage.

Socialize and win people over.

2 What works for a child will not work for an adult — give it up.

3 If you can lose all childishness, you will be given more responsibilities and the achievements that go along with them. Get noticed, and be consistent.

4 Following may generate successes but only to a point. Thereafter you must rely on your own instincts and intuitions, and learn to trust yourself.

5 You become like whatever you follow. Following excellence, you receive the confidence you need, wisdom sinks in and achievement follows you.

6 We also become bound to whatever or whoever we follow and must adhere to the rules.

A noble leader, attuned to the need for sacrifice and worship (possibly in the west or on a mountain or both), gains blessings for both himself and his followers.

Hexagram 18
The Obsolete

The Statement

Dealing with what no longer works requires determination. What worked in your parents' time may be wrong now.

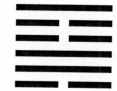

Think it over for a brief period (perhaps three days), then get to it. It will require about as long to act as it has to consider.

The Lines

1 From birth we follow our parents, learn to speak and walk from them. Their genes, personalities and prejudices naturally become our first identity.

A father's shortcomings must be examined and managed, however difficult. At last, this leads to good fortune.

2 The more passive parent's problems (traditionally, the mother's) can be handled gently.

3 It is very rare that the problems of an aging or recently deceased father figure are not inherited, to some extent, by the surviving family members. This must be dealt with but there is no blame in it.

4 When you know that an attitude, a habit or even a business inherited from a father figure is obsolete, allowing it to continue will only bring more trouble.

If the problem is more like a genetic disorder, the outlook is similarly unfortunate.

5 Whether you are dealing with the decline of a father figure, funeral arrangements or an estate problem, an honorable course is always available and in this case, will be appreciated by others.

Whatever your own concerns, there is a fair and honorable course, and that is what you should choose.

6 Here you have transcended the obsolete and the mundane. You may set the highest goals for yourself, with very good prospects.

This is a wonderful line for beginning a spiritual path or quest, or confidently breaking with any constraints of your past.

Hexagram 19
Conduct

The Statement

Sometimes called Approach or Arrival, there are basically
no negative lines in this hexagram, and the assumption
is that whatever you are undertaking can meet with
success, so long as you are receptive to others and actively
generous with your finest qualities and best conduct.

But the time may not last long. Tradition has it that in the eighth month (perhaps
August for an American, or in the Chinese calendar, the period between mid-
September and mid-October), misfortune will occur.

The Lines

1 Partners or friends arrive and you can work with them to produce wonderful
results.

2 The outlook is about the same as line one, but you may have moved even further
along with a very successful partnership.

3 You cannot just be carried away by the times, however promising. You must
examine yourself and your undertaking and your companions, to be sure that
complacency, nepotism, or laziness have not slipped into the mix.

4 Here you have arrived at your goal and there is nothing wrong with that. The
higher the goal, the better the result will be. This can be an excellent spiritual
auspice.

5 There is a kind of well earned and deeply considered wisdom or spiritual
satisfaction here, and a successful undertaking with others.

6 The openhearted, generous and sincere pursuit of this matter gets good results
at this time. It is possible that you have arrived at a transcendent realization,
spiritually, and you may even consider teaching what you've learned, if other
indications support this plan. The choice is yours.

Hexagram 20
Overview

The Statement

The preparations have been made, but the crucial thing remains undone.

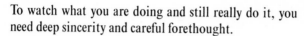

It is like the moment in a ceremony just before an offering is made.

To watch what you are doing and still really do it, you need deep sincerity and careful forethought.

Ideally, this is like Pavarotti, in his prime, singing Puccini, or Aretha Franklin singing Amazing Grace, a unity of deep feeling and impeccable performance.

The ancient spiritual kings moved far and wide to make their assessments and present true teachings.

The Lines

1 A childlike view is fine for a child, but a sophisticated person will only look foolish trying to imitate that.

2 Playing "I Spy" with others' lives is not a very useful tool, unless it's the only one available to you and the matter is worth feeling a little underhanded about. It is probably better to take a passive course.

3 Reflect a while and get a little distance from this matter. Then look down upon your life situation as an angelic spirit might. This kind of overview can tell you whether to go forward or go back.

4 Consider the nation's true glory – that may be a useful exercise. Otherwise take optimal advantage of your relations with, or a visit to, someone of influence and authority.

5 Take stock of your life and identify your real faults and problems, so you can get rid of them.

6 Consider the overview of Jesus, Gandhi, the Buddha or another sage or saint that you may identify with, and emulate the example. You should always look to this high standard to measure yourself, and, where necessary, to make a judgment of others.

Hexagram 21

Cut To It

The Statement

You must penetrate the situation as if biting into tough meat.

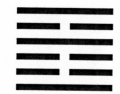

The prosecution of wrongdoing may be called for and punishment may be applied.

Once judgment is clear, the verdict can be lightning fast.

The Lines

1 In the harshest ancient days, to be put in stocks and have your toes cut off was considered a fairly light punishment. In this case neither the infraction nor the reprimand is excessive.

2 The idea of loss of face was quite literal in the feudal past, a nose might be cut off.

The punishment may be more metaphorical today, but is nonetheless painful.

3 Here we have the idea of biting tough meat and encountering poison: a hidden problem is uncovered in the ordinary course of things.

It is regrettable but most likely unavoidable.

4 Cutting through is tough but rewarding. Grit and integrity pay off, as if by accident, like cutting away rock and finding a vein of gold.

5 The task is hard, but if you keep at it there will be a good outcome, possibly exceeding your expectations.

6 This is the line of the *really* hard case, deaf to wisdom, unwilling to heed warnings and punished very severely. If it is you, wise up.

If it is somebody else, rest assured that justice will come down like a hammer.

Hexagram 22
Elegance

The Statement

Graceful adornments speak of a high culture, on a personal and a social level. An elegant bearing indicates that things are going well, but elegance itself accomplishes only fairly small, superficial things.

Confucius is supposed to have been distressed when he got this reading concerning his work on the *I Ching*. Perhaps it did not suit his sense of profundity.

There is another way to look at it, however, which is that a considerable state of grace must already exist before elegance is even a consideration; so good fortune is already manifest in our surroundings and our person, and that is certainly nothing to take for granted.

It is not the time for great undertakings, however, or the time to underestimate the importance of even somewhat superficial concerns.

The Lines

1 Even if your shoes are stylish, you should be able to walk in them. Someone leaves a vehicle to go on foot. Perhaps it is time to forego ease for some more rewarding consideration, or perhaps a necessary change will be easier to make than was thought.

2 Even a haircut or a beard trim can have a positive influence at times, but a preoccupation with such things is, of course, mere vanity, unworthy of a lot of consideration.

3 Inner beauty overwhelms superficial concerns, and that is what should be relied upon.

4 Dazzling beauty can put you off or intimidate you, if you are not careful. Don't miss a good partner just because they knock you out so much that it's a little scary.

If your question is of a spiritual nature, the symbol is that of a white feathered horse. This is a powerfully favorable sign.

5 You may lack the resources or looks you desire. So what?

That is all skin deep and temporary, anyway. Do what you can, sincerely, and all will be well.

6 At some moments like this you may seem to have it all, elegance, grace, serenity. No one can find fault with that.

Hexagram 23
Top Heavy

The Statement

Ambition, pride or a control freak pushes things too far.

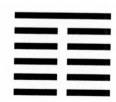

The competition to build ever taller Gothic Cathedrals in the Renaissance finally pushed beyond the limits of the available technology, and the ornate churches sometimes collapsed, killing hundreds of the faithful inside.

This situation is also like the Tower card in Tarot, which I presume has its origins in the biblical (or Sumerian) story of the Tower of Babel.

There is no gain here and whether it is the nature of the times, or poor character is to blame, things are coming apart. Collapse is imminent.

The best way to weather such times is to practice generosity and honesty. If you see a crack, point it out, and run.

Things could get worse before they get better.

The Lines

1 Maybe it doesn't look so bad yet. Do not be fooled into further action, the rug is about to be pulled out from under you.

2 Even more clear signs of collapse are evident. You can see and hear the tower cracking. Get out of the way, if you can.

3 Sometimes something must be torn down, in which case you may as well assist in the process.

Other times they just come down, as in a mudslide. Either way it is not your fault.

4 A place of comfort and rest is ruined and it is quite unfortunate. Traditionally, a bed is split apart.

5 A good exit strategy may dawn on you, or simple good luck can appear in a time of general chaos, and this is extremely fortunate for you and all your relations, a stroke of divine intervention, apparently.

6 A time of collapse indicates good fortune for the masterful and disaster for the foolish. The Oracle evidently suggests that you make all possible efforts to be masterful.

Time will tell.

Hexagram 24
Returning

The Statement

They say it is darkest before the dawn, or maybe it only seems so because we have grown tired of waiting. Here, the waiting is nearly over and before long (traditionally seven days) you can move ahead.

But soon does not mean right now. Calmly prepare and you'll be able to see when the dawning light is sufficiently bright for a return to normal.

The Lines

1 Having only ventured, or strayed, a short distance, it is easy enough to return.

Good fortune.

2 Take a break, and then return; this is best now.

3 This return may be dangerous, either because it has already been done so often, or because of the urgency of the situation. Be extra careful.

4 Sometimes a return to right behavior or a more balanced approach is a lonely course of action.

Maybe no one else gets it that you are on the right path.

5 A return to the highest of values is nothing to regret and you will not be blamed for it.

6 This situation is a like a disastrous retreat. Napoleon and Hitler made the same tactical mistake when attacking Russia with winter coming on and winter, as much as the opposing army, decimated them. Custer could not escape from his ill-conceived raid at the Little Big Horn, and his legendary swagger was of no use when the real situation dawned on him, too late to return to safety.

Hexagram 25
Innocence

The Statement

Innocence, like youthful vitality, is a desirable state, but it confers no special immunity if it leads, even innocently, into danger or wrong behavior.

So, while the signs are for success and good fortune, they are not automatic and conduct must be good to assure that misfortune does not creep into the situation.

The most simple answer to a problem is probably the best one, if you are sifting through possible courses of action.

The Lines

1 Simple innocence brings good fortune.

2 Sometimes, plain old good timing is worth more than all the work and planning you could possibly do.

3 Bad luck can be so infuriating when you can see the good fortune so close by that might, it seems, have been yours.

Someone else will win it, though, and this will test your heart's innocence.

4 This is the "Try, try again" line. There is, of course, no blame attached to this.

5 If you have done no wrong, then just let things run their course without interference.

(Traditionally: "Take no medicine for an illness you did not bring on yourself.")

6 This may be the "No good deed goes unpunished" line. Or it may simply mean that a perfectly blameless course of action backfires, so if it hasn't already happened, don't bother, at this time.

Hexagram 26
Harnessed Power

The Statement

Power must be focused or restrained, and then released wisely. This is as true of a person as it is in the case of a race horse, a dam feeding water to a turbine, or the investment of your cash flow.

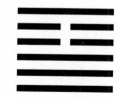

You may need to get out and travel a bit, but large undertakings will be possible.

Look to the patterns of past history and prophecy for clues to success and do not neglect your spiritual study.

The Lines

1 Sometimes events conspire to create a dangerous blockage on your path, so you must stop or else the logjam will surely cause misfortune.

2 Another kind of misfortune occurs when the axle of your vehicle is broken and you are involuntarily stopped in your tracks.

3 If your vehicle is in good shape you can go forward, but it is still up to you to do the driving.

Maintain things diligently all day long and guard against accidents. It also helps to know exactly where you want to go.

4 A bull in a china shop, of course, creates havoc. Restrain the bull well ahead of time and a good result is assured.

5 If the wild force of the situation is controlled like that of a gelded animal, you can expect a favorable outcome.

6 Sometimes, when all the necessary restraints and guidance systems are ingeniously placed, and all power is being put to its best use, it is like being on a road to heaven, or a rocket to the stars, perhaps. All you have to do now is continue.

Hexagram 27
Good Food and Good Company

The Statement

Everybody who is healthy likes to nosh and talk a bit. It is nothing but fortunate to enjoy good nourishment and a nice gathering.

But in eating, as with speaking, there are acceptable and unacceptable ways to employ the mouth. Nobody likes a gross pig at a social meal and nobody wants to sit next to a loud-mouthed bore at any gathering. Take care in what you choose to eat and what you choose to say.

The Lines

1 The most ancient origins of the *I Ching* involved reading the cracks of a magic (or divine) tortoise's shell.

Here you have your own version of the divine turtle at hand but you look away, to watch another chewing food. Are you jealous, confused or what?

The very act of mistrusting what you already had brings misfortune.

2 The Emerald City is run by a fast talking sham, not a wonderful Wizard of Oz. The grass is not greener on the far side of the hill. The wealth that others may have, deservedly or not, is really none of your business.

Don't talk yourself into going away from the good nourishment nearby, or grouse about doing the honest work required to obtain it.

3 Spiteful arguments are a poor use of the mouth, and even if you are not altogether at fault, the result is bad. Try to return to what really nourishes you.

4 Here a tiger's style of hunting and eating are indicated.

Your action may border on the wild, but it is appropriate to the situation.

5 Maybe you have a weight problem or caffeine issue, maybe it is just too much mental junk food, or you talk too much. Anyway, it is a manageable problem. Whatever it is, get it under control before you try anything too big.

6 Though times are tough, you can find or have already stored enough nourishment for yourself and others to make it through, and this is very admirable.

Hexagram 28
In Excess

The Statement

A sagging beam is pictured, but it has not yet broken under the strain. Some aspect of the situation is dangerously excessive, yet with careful attention to the imbalance   success is quite possible. You may continue.

The Lines

1 A mat of straw, sandbags, thick blankets of encouragement, whatever you've got, should be employed to cautiously shore things up and avoid a mistake.

2 Sometimes, just when things look sure to fail, a sudden resurgence of good fortune shows up, to great advantage. There is life in the old boy, yet.

3 Here the weight, or imbalance, is overwhelming and of such instability, that misfortune cannot be avoided.

4 A crown beam here is unusually strong and it will hold unless there has been sabotage. In any case, it is your task to trust in the fundamental strength of your position and stay cool. Things will likely turn out well.

5 A few weak signs of unexpected vitality or resilience are not enough to bet very much on. A little inconsequential luck comes, at best, but a small and wasted effort is equally possible.

6 We know a bit more about the tectonic and aquatic mechanics of a Tsunami today than the ancients probably did, but not enough to keep people from being submerged, pushed helplessly along and killed by them. Such waves are still terrifying and beyond human control.

Still, some people will go under and fight through to the other side, basically unharmed. That is all you can hope for here, to be one of those people, because at the moment, you are in danger of being swept away.

Hexagram 29
The Chasm

The Statement

A chasm with water flowing through it is inherently dangerous on a journey.

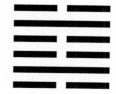

Your situation will require utmost skill and sincerity.

Tie your very being to what is right and move ahead with honor.

A master will see the pitfalls immediately and give critical instructions to others.

The Lines

1 Sometimes there is a chasm hidden within a chasm; misfortune.

2 This pit has dangers that nobody can see and even the I Ching cannot explain very much about it to you, at present. It goes without saying that if you are not yet in the pit, don't go there.

3 This is like jumping into a chasm to avoid something that is chasing you, but it will be of no use – it is a nightmare scenario, to be avoided at all costs.

4 While you are waiting for a way out, someone brings you food and drink; this bolsters your hopes and in the end there is nothing to blame yourself about.

5 You are in a flooding cave but the water has not yet reached the top. You can still get out.

6 This is a terrifying line, so if you are asking about something you have not yet done, in the name of all divine tortoises, don't do it.

If it is too late, then it will be a long, unhappy time before you can tear free of this chasm.

Hexagram 30
Brightness

The Statement

You can watch the flowers in a field turn toward the light to be nourished, over the course of a day.

You can tell a lot about a person by their turning toward enlightenment, over the course of a lifetime.

The ancients saw the benefits of both the light and the heat of a fire as a unity of blessing. Some early civilizations worshiped the sun and, societies in general have seen the quality of brightness as a superior sign. The hero is often depicted in a mystical glow and when someone is smart, we say they are bright.

The ultimate scientific measure of things has turned out to be the speed of light but even as we clock it, brightness remains a spiritual mystery as in the statement Jesus made, "I am the light of the world."

So, whatever your question, this hexagram predicts a brilliant illumination of the situation.

An essential docility, likened traditionally to a woman caring for a cow, is the modest perseverance that brings success, but the influence is potentially widespread and fortunate, as well.

The Lines

1. You may not see the way yet, but if you go forward with sincerity, things will be all right.

2 This is a very auspicious line, as brightness has become full and remained modest at the same time. Good fortune

3 The sun also sets, and no amount of incantation will bring it back until dawn.

When the sun sets on a great person's life in old age, what is there to do but sigh and acknowledge that there is sometimes misfortune. Don't dwell on it.

4 A sudden, possibly very destructive blaze is also bright, but usually best buried and forgotten as soon as it goes out.

5 This line is about expressing deep grief and sorrow, and for some reason in this case, it will bring good fortune.

Perhaps it is cathartic, perhaps another needs to see it, perhaps it is a sign of spiritual growth – it depends on the situation.

6 Brightness can even extend to a situation of forceful action. Fairness and compassion toward those we have defeated sets the stage for a more illumined future relationship. It is also possible that you will have to call someone on their nonsense, but there is no use being self-righteous about it.

Hexagram 31
Attraction

The Statement

The attraction of romantic love overwhelms almost everyone sometime, so the Oracle (and all societies) counsel with rules for correct behavior in courtship. Most of us are biologically hardwired to participate, and psychologically hard pressed to understand even our own, let alone our partners', deepest needs and motivations. Good luck with all that.

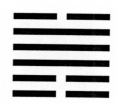

But all kinds of openhearted attraction to others are favored at this moment.

The Lines

1 Here one is getting a tingling feeling, as if in the toes, which has not yet turned into forward motion. No auspice is attached to this, as nothing much has happened yet.

2 Here the legs seem to want to move ahead on their own, but the time is not right.

Stay put.

3 It may be (and I am really fishing here) that the ancient view was that what becomes sexual desire comes from the toes on up. In any case, the urge to go ahead has now reached the thighs, but it is still not the right time to act, and persistence will fail, badly.

4 Now the time is right and success is virtually guaranteed, but you must move ahead decisively, or only your closest friends will support you.

5 Everyone from an accomplished yogi to a kid watching an adventure movie knows what a spine-tingling feeling is about. There is nothing wrong with pursuing that kind of sensation just now. If you are already experiencing such exhilaration, the situation is just fine.

6 Here the attraction has reached the point of expression. Romantic words may be spoken or a first kiss might be stolen.

Exasperatingly, no particular significance is assigned to this, but we may assume a kind of silent assent to our expression, after all the previous warnings and all the buildup.

Or perhaps the Oracle simply knows that in romance, you are on your own.

If your question is not of a romantic nature, it is time to verbalize your intentions in another matter.

Hexagram 32
Stability

The Statement

What in this world has unassailable stability? Only change.

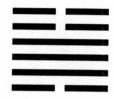

But people long for stability and strive to keep it.

In human affairs, to keep our promises, to move ahead with strong moral convictions, to have compassion and an enduring sense of direction – these things will bring success.

The Lines

1 To try to enforce stability in an unstable situation brings misfortune. There is no gain there.

2 You can stop worrying about this one, your regrets will disappear.

3 You or someone else has been too inconsistent at times and some trust is lost. Of course this leads to regret.

4 Like a hunter who wanders into a place where there is no game, there is no use looking for stability in a circumstance that cannot offer it.

5 A passive response gets a good result, aggressiveness doesn't.

6 Too much attachment to a status quo or too much reliance on the value of conformity is not the way.

Neither is a neurotic agitation toward change for its own sake. There is misfortune inherent in all such emotional excesses.

Hexagram 33
Retreat

The Statement

Go back, retreat and look for small gains at best.

Stay cool and keep your distance from those you do not trust, but be polite about it.

The Lines

1 The tail end of a retreat is where the enemy is most likely to catch up to you and harm you. Your position is not good.

2 Being held, as if tied, to a successful retreat, is an acceptable, safe, but hardly victorious position.

3 A hasty retreat involves sacrifices, like the loss of everything that cannot be easily carried and perhaps, a lapse in healthful and balanced behavior, So people must be reminded to get hold of themselves, and do their duty. Otherwise illness and chaos could cause more harm than the enemy.

4 When retreat is the only course, the wise will benefit and those who lose their heads will certainly suffer. Plan ahead, stay cool and be ready to move out.

5 Here a retreat is carried out in an excellent manner. It is like the brilliant chess move that leads, later, to a possible victory.

6 All that is really important has been brought along with you in this case, and the retreat is more like a voluntary relocation, with all your goods intact.

In spiritual terms, one may be ready to retire from the world.

Hexagram 34
A Position of Strength

The Statement

A strong heart vigorously circulates the blood that nourishes the entire body, and it becomes strong.

A strong leader moves the necessary benefits to all the people and the nation stands in a position of strength.

Creative action is favored and there is support at this time for accomplishing your goals.

The Lines

1 At the very beginning of an enterprise, too much force stumbles and fails, as if the toes were trying to independently move the whole body. You trip. Right yourself and wait for complete readiness.

2 We must begin, of course, with a single step, and should continue only when our coordination is steady. Then there can be a good outcome.

3 People often say work smart, not hard. This is not the time to bull ahead without careful consideration of the task at hand. You will only get your horns tangled in a fence.

4 Helpers with cutting tools can open the way for you now, or punch a hole in something that has had you walled in, and you will proceed with your power intact.

5 You or another can easily lose some stubborn bullheadedness now, and relax. Good.

Calmly stand down.

6 This is one more situation where the harder you struggle, the more entrapped you become, but relief is on the way, once the urge to struggle is worn out.

Hexagram 35
Progress

The Statement

The time of troubles has come to an end, with gifts and praise surrounding your success.

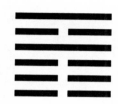

A leader assures you of his blessings more than once; the keys to his house and cars are yours for the asking.

As a matter of course, you should think seriously about the qualities you had to acquire to get here.

The Lines

1 Something halts the happy proceedings. Maybe someone does not trust you, as yet. Be good natured and compassionate about it.

2 The situation worries you, but steadiness will win the day.

You may receive blessings from an older woman, perhaps your grandmother.

3 Your inner circle is loyal and you seem to be a crowd pleaser. This will go a long way to smooth over any problems or regrets. Good fortune.

4 If you progress like a rat stuffing his mouth, greedy and restless, you will be seen and avoided as such.

5 Sometimes things get so good spiritually and materially, that one can transcend even the idea of loss and gain.

The phrase "It's all good" is actually true in this situation.

6 Unfortunately, a lot of progress comes on the heels of conflict and aggression.

If it is unavoidable, then let it be as brief as possible.

Hexagram 36
The Dying of the Light

The Statement

The brightness and progress of former times is fading away. But your inner light need not be extinguished by mere circumstances.

Darkness and ignorance are an injury to all and point toward bewildering adversity.

But inner light can persist and survive because it exists within. In the end, it is beyond all tyrants' powers, even death.

The Lines

1 The struggle brings weariness and deprivation. Sometimes it is best to fast briefly or do without any comforts, and focus only on what must be done. Soon (in perhaps three days), you will reach your destination.

2 The darkness brings an injury (perhaps in the left thigh, or something interferes with your ability to receive help). But someone of extraordinary strength (or perhaps a heroic effort on your own part) comes to the rescue. Things end better than may have seemed possible.

3 Napoleon was thwarted and incarcerated a number of times, but he kept coming back with a new army to raise hell again. You cannot nullify the influence of a wily opponent with a single act of containment; to establish a new order takes longer than one successful campaign. So be patient as well as persistent.

4 The heart of darkness lies at the end of a trail of darkness. The act of removing such a heart requires surgical efficiency along with a very deft logistic approach and a practical escape plan. This is like a very dangerous Special Ops maneuver, to search out and destroy some hidden darkness.

5 Sometimes there is nothing to do but to act so crazy or stupid that the tyrants will see you as too unimportant to destroy. Meanwhile, you can begin to take steps in secret.

6 After falling to the depths of darkness from a high place, it may even be necessary to go underground, in complete darkness, to survive.

Another interpretation of this line is that one who was high and mighty has had a Humpty Dumpty fall and will end up in the earth (presumably dead or at least powerless).

Either interpretation might be right, I think, depending on the question.

Hexagram 37
Family

The Statement

In family matters, it is the feminine way that brings the best benefits. Nurturing, nourishing, and remaining constant in affection and love are the ideals.

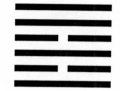

But a father speaks when it is necessary to speak, and stands prepared to meet the outside world.

The Lines

1 At home with the family, the cares of the world and its woes can disappear, at least for a little while.

2 Staying home and doing a little cooking, or getting a little home-style specialty from mom may be the just what the doctor ordered at present. The woman of the house has special significance, here, and household responsibilities are favored.

3 Of course, if the atmosphere becomes too yin or lax and playful, dad may have to step in and lay down the law.

4 If your family is well off and generous toward you, you can't beat that.

5 You can withdraw into a very well off and secure family situation like a fortress, and you will need no other help.

6 You may be working on something with only your family's support, and maybe nobody even gets what you are doing, yet. Maintain your dignity and work hard; you won't let them down.

Exemplary work succeeds.

Hexagram 38
Alienation

The Statement

People are at odds over great matters and opposition rules, at the moment.

But there is a charm and attraction in the small things that people have in common, which could begin to heal the rifts.

This is what all the idiotic baby kissing and eating at local diners is about in a political campaign. You must not lose yourself in such a process; still, small gestures begin the communication that leads to healing, and opposition must not tempt you away from generous values.

The Lines

1 Loss can be regained and quickly, if you don't make a big deal out of it.

Still, be very cautious with those you know are in the wrong, or whose intentions are suspect.

2 Do not brush brusquely past someone you meet as if by chance, say, in a hallway. He may be the master, come to check on your own worthiness. Awareness of this encounter results in an acknowledgement that you are not to blame for this time of alienation.

3 Loss of face, demotion and humiliation are coming now, but there will be a different, happier ending to this story after some time has passed.

4 Alienated and alone, you meet a like-minded individual who will turn out to be quite powerful. Share your vision with this person and despite the severe conditions of the present, a better future may come.

5 Opposition and difficulty disappear. Your family or close associates bite through opposition as easily as if it were the skin of a piece of fried chicken.

You may proceed confidently.

6 Prolonged opposition can make us so guarded that we can become paranoid.

Are we being attacked by spirits or wild animals barely seen in a foggy drizzle?

We draw our weapon.

No, it is not an enemy but a close friend whom we have had trouble making out in the rain.

Meet the gentle rain, meet the friend, and meet your long awaited fortune.

Hexagram 39
Troubles

The Statement

Zorba the Greek told his young friend: "Life is trouble, only death is no trouble."

One possible response would have been: "Yes, but some times in life are more trouble than others."

This is such a situation. It is also like being boxed in by troubles and instead of having a lot of options, perhaps there is only one narrow route of escape, if that (traditionally in the southwest).

As usual, the Oracle recommends that inward-turning contemplation offers the best hope of finding the character traits needed to resolve your difficulties. This may be a frustrating thing to hear in the midst of a crisis, but it is an unavoidable lesson of life.

The Lines

1 Action is not favored, but honor may come to you if you remain still.

2 If you are in the service of others who are in trouble, some of the trouble will fall on you, although you are not to blame and seem duty bound to proceed regardless.

3 Pushing ahead will only lead to worse troubles, so return to your friends and wait for change to swing back your way.

4 Again pressing on is not favored, but it may be possible to begin forging useful alliances with those you already know.

5 You are pretty well screwed in your current position, but as the situation reaches its worst, friends arrive. It is like the old western movie scenario where you are surrounded and at the last moment the cavalry charges in to the rescue.

6 Let's say your car breaks down, you are broke, and your cell phone is dead. It's way too far to walk anywhere that will do you any good, and so you sit under a tree to meditate. A wise man appears to you in a vision and smiles. You feel better.

A motorist stops and asks if you need any help. He gives you a ride home and you offer him whatever change you have in your pocket for gas, but he waves you off.

As he drives away you check and find you don't have any change in your pocket. You have a winning lottery ticket that will cover the cost of your car repair.

Hexagram 40
Relief

The Statement

The way a good rain relieves a drought, the way a hiking companion might release us from a thicket of brambles into which we have stumbled, we are about to be freed from former troubles that held us hostage.

Escape, quickness and a return to safe haven (traditionally in the southwest) are indicated.

The Lines

1 Victims frequently feel guilty about their former misfortunes. Don't.

You have done nothing wrong.

2 Humans have learned a lot from foxes about cleverness in hunting. Here you catch three foxes on your own, and your skills are recognized. You may receive a valuable gift of three golden arrows (a big deal in bronze age terms – or even now, come to think of it), for your considerable merit. Continue on.

3 You could plunge right back into trouble by showing off now. Adopt the most humble position you can or you may get ripped off, just because you seem to have something that others want.

4 I have never understood this line. It has to do with the removing of one's own toes

(don't try this one at home, kids) and thereafter, friends arrive.

It may be possible that after much effort we have only managed to untie the bonds on our toes, but thereafter friends show up and release us, Walker, Texas Ranger-style.

Just a guess.

5 To free yourself or others is a major accomplishment and commands the respect of all concerned. To then make sure that such entanglement cannot happen again, is the mark of a true leader.

6 Once released from your bonds, you can set higher goals and make use of your skills to considerable, even thrilling advantage. The traditional image is to take aim at a hawk on a high wall and hit your mark.

Hexagram 41
Decrease

The Statement

It probably bears comment that in the psychology of the American Dream increase is the preeminent motivation. Bigger is better and all that.

But decrease of rain in a deluge or decrease of eating in obesity are clearly positive, decrease of pain is almost always good.

Money may be tight now or some other shortage may be occurring but you can still find positive things to do, like decrease your anger and modify your appetites to accommodate the times.

If you offer even something as small as a roadside flower to the master with sincerity, his heart will break with love for you.

The Lines

1 Take care of business as quickly as you can and don't waste time creating busy work.

2 You cannot build anything useful without the needed materials, except patience and acceptance. These will make you a better craftsman when the time comes.

3 Three's a crowd, in this situation, whereas holding your own, ironically, may attract exactly the helper you need.

4 A quick identification of some personal problem, such as a prejudice, phobia or neurosis, and equally swift action to correct it, will bring you joy.

Do not give in to hatred of any kind; get above the problem.

5 Tortoise shells, in addition to their use in divination, were also used as money in ancient days, and no one can stop the good fortune that is coming your way now, whether it is of a spiritual or monetary nature. Ten bundles of tortoise shells.

That's a lot of wampum, boys.

6 You may find increase in a time of general decrease. If others have not been deprived in the process, there is certainly no harm in that. You may acquire helpers, but nothing as substantial as a home.

Hexagram 42
Increase

The Statement

You can advance now, and even quite difficult enterprises are generally favored. This is not merely true of something like the work needed to extract wealth from a newly found vein in a gold mine, it is equally true of working to refine the inner self to create a heart of gold.

The Lines

1 Great work should equal great fortune, here. It is largely up to you, but a wily element of luck is not altogether settled, as yet, so stay on guard.

2 This is one of the most fortunate lines in the I Ching. Everything, it seems, is going your way and your opponents are powerless. Obviously, this is also an appropriate time to give thanks.

3 This line reminds me of those jobs where something has to go wrong before you are needed, like a tow truck driver or an EMT. If you are such a person, you are going to be making a lot of overtime now.

If you are not in such a line, you can expect to receive increase through something unfortunate, and while it is unsettling, you need to remain blameless, centered and be prepared to explain whatever you understand about the situation to those with a right to know. It could be something as simple as a larger than expected insurance settlement.

4 Here you are a subordinate in a major undertaking and as long as your advice is moderate and well considered, it will be followed to success.

5 Thus far you have been so generous and kindhearted in your conduct that it is hardly necessary to consult the oracle. Good fortune and recognition.

6 Increase can lead to self-centeredness, which can lead to greed and hard heartedness, which leads to a downfall without a single ally to call on, in the end. Misfortune.

Hexagram 43
The Activist

The Statement

You have a pretty good idea of what is going on and who or what is to blame. That is the easy part.

The tricky, and historically sometimes lethal part, is to align with the wise and powerful, inform them of the gravity of the situation and persuade them to take decisive action before it is too late. To do this, you must take decisive action yourself.

When you win, let all who helped share in the glory.

The Lines

1 B.B. King has a song called "Never Make Your Move Too Soon", and he knows what he is talking about. If you do move too soon, you will be swept aside as a foolish upstart.

2 Make your case and ask for help. Secretive moves may be made against you, or night time fighting may seem to go on and on, but you can emerge unscathed.

3 You may have to stand alone, or walk alone in the midst of derision and humiliation.

You have chosen this path and only time will tell if you were right.

4 Even as you are humiliated you will be offered a way out, but you are probably too bull headed to take it, because it requires following someone else's lead which you seem very much disinclined to do, or even to listen to. Sometimes even a fierce activist needs to stand down, to fight another day.

5 In volatile times, traitors or troubles grow like weeds and must be cleared away with the same determination.

6 This is, hands down, the scariest line in the I Ching, to me.

In the end, misfortune comes without warning.

A traitor has gone unnoticed until it is too late, possibly.

But any number of other unforeseeable misfortunes could be indicated, depending on the nature of your question.

Hexagram 44

Intercourse

The Statement

The woman is too powerful for a productive union. It is not the attraction, but the entanglement that is dangerous. The warning could be reversed and as easily be meant for a woman, I think, as tradition applies it to a man.

In any other situation, someone who is overly ambitious or unscrupulous tries to infiltrate the established order and must not be allowed to do so.

The Lines

1 Do not take the turn down lover's lane. Put on the brakes, get out, and fling yourself into a muddy ditch. You will be better off in the long run.

But there is very little chance that you will heed this advice, and misfortune comes as a result of unrestrained continuation of a wrong course of action.

2 You have enough for yourself, but it is not time to try to entertain others, or expect them to entertain you. Keep a cool distance.

3 Having been rebuffed or even punished, you may not have been at fault, but you should have enough sense to back off now.

4 There is nothing here but wrapping paper. Party's over, go home.

5 The sweetness of the unexpected, like maybe an encounter with someone you thought did not care for you but, it turns out, is as infatuated as you are.

If it is not a romantic situation, it could be a windfall or some other unexpected and very welcome benefit.

6 Elk and rams butting horns to attract a mate, or bellowing gorillas may be back there in our genetic conditioning, but it hasn't worked out very well for the last few thousand years in human society, as a technique for successful courtship. (Spring Break, Mardi Gras and certain rural counties which I will not name, being possible exceptions).

In fact, the point of social refinement in romance is to control the wild, primal desire that may reside in the subconscious.

Another possible interpretation of this line is that you may be in a state of aggressive sexual obsession, or another kind of aggression. Either way, misfortune for the aggressive.

Hexagram 45

Gathering

The Statement

People gather for all kinds of purposes, political, religious, general entertainments, or business conventions and clearly some basic order must have already been established for these kinds of events to come off successfully.

In ancient times, the Emperor and his priests were the only show in town for the most part, but all kinds of social bonds were reinforced in their seasonal rituals. The times now favor gatherings to accomplish pretty much the same feelings of unity and fraternity as in days of old.

It is also a good time to check out the effectiveness of the current leadership and get a sense of which way the winds of change are blowing. Pay attention and gain fortune.

The Lines

1 Some gatherings are just a mess, like a rigged election or a family reunion where different cliques simply will not associate with each other. It's not your fault and in time, folks will see that. At least you did what you could to help, until you simply had to leave.

2 Other gatherings sometimes go as if they were planned for you personally. A small offering is enthusiastically received and good fortune follows.

3 Gatherings such as funerals are sad and can often be quite awkward as well, especially if you had little emotional connection to the deceased. Don't beat yourself up about it.

If your presence is required at some unfamiliar event, the word is *decorum*. This means do a little research on the etiquette of how things are usually handled in this kind of situation and play your part as best you can.

4 A spontaneous blow out to celebrate someone's sudden success (maybe your own) is a great, fun thing, just don't go overboard.

5 Here there is a gathering around some big shot who actually deserves his status. There is always some grumbling and mistrust somewhere at such a powerful gathering. Be sincere, friendly and open.

6 There are lots of ways for things to go very wrong in a time of gathering. Whatever it is, it could have a negative effect on you, even though it is no way your fault.

Take a pass, if you can.

Hexagram 46
Rise Above

The Statement

This is a time to grow and act, climbing the ladder of success, and seeking the advice and help of the wisest and most powerful people you know.

Don't try to skip steps or forget that the tallest tree was once a seed.

But you are no longer like a sapling or a child, and you have climbed long enough to have hit your stride with confidence.

Advance to fortune.

The Lines

1. Your own confidence is met with that of those around you. Move on up.

2 The summer (solstice) sacrifice was perhaps the most important of the year, in that it was meant to ensure the harvest which people relied upon to survive the winter.

Here you are told to trust in the summer sacrifice, and by extension, have faith in the Tao, God, your higher power or Guru, to receive the blessings you seek.

3 Here you rise into an empty city. Are your goals worthwhile? Are your methods sound?

Are you being lured into a trap? Or is it just that easy? You must look and see.

4 A basic human desire to rise above has accompanied every important scientific and spiritual advancement in the history of the world. You are rising and rewards are coming.

Do not be afraid of bold innovation. The Wright brothers and the guys who built the pyramids were putting their butts out there, in a big way.

Do not be ashamed of traditional spiritual reverence, either.

5 Step by step, as if in a procession to meet a dignitary, that is the way now.

6 Here is an image of rising at night, or in darkness.

Ray Charles went all over the world and even if he had, perhaps, to step a little more determinedly than somebody else, it didn't seem to slow him down much.

Hexagram 47
Worn Out

The Statement

Everything wears out eventually and here many things may be at an all time low for you.

Money, health, luck, even your welcome may be wearing thin.

It may be time to see the doctor, spiritual teacher, shaman, banker or some other person with special skills or resources to help you through.

At the same time, people's trust may have worn thin, as well.

Thomas Jefferson went bankrupt once and was, for all practical purposes, bankrupt again at the time of his death. Edison failed to find the filament for his electric light for so long that it nearly ruined his credibility with everyone he knew, and his investors were flipping out.

Sometimes you have to risk everything to prevail, and exhaustion can happen to the best of us.

The Lines

1 In a ruined forest, you wander for a long time without relief. No help.

2 You have what you need, for the moment, but trouble is coming and you need to get spiritually centered and meet it straight on. You cannot run away from this.

3 You are in deep trouble and perhaps unable or unwilling to take even comfort from the person closest to you.

(Traditionally, after an excruciating ordeal a man enters his palace, only to discover that he cannot find his wife.)

4 Here things begin to improve slowly, and you have both a suitable vehicle for escape and an end to your troubles.

5 Punishing times and bad relations with those in authority are upon you. Be willing to give some things up and start negotiating.

6 If we have taken a disastrous course, then suffering the result is bad enough, without sinking into depression about it as well. Resolve not to make these mistakes again, get hold of yourself, and move on.

Hexagram 48
The Well

The Statement

You can move a city, but the spring that feeds a well stays where it is.

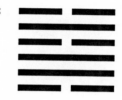

You draw from it, and the level stays the same.

A poor man can take a cup, the same as a rich man.

But if your rope is too short or your bucket has a hole in it, the best well is of no use to you.

The Lines

1 Once the water of a well is fouled or the spring has gone dry, no one can be refreshed there anymore. This well is done.

2 If a lake or river has connected with the spring, the purity of the water is gone and carp swim about in it.. A cracked bucket is not much use, either. Your source has been compromised.

3 Pure water sometimes lies just a little deeper than the muck in evidence here. The Oracle is saddened that a fine source of refreshment (perhaps spiritual) is not being used. This is possibly for lack of effort or just plain ignorance. Take the hint and dig a little deeper or encourage others to do so.

4 Maintenance, like the laying of a brick enclosure, may make a well unusable, but only briefly, until the work is done, then it is as good as ever.

5 You have found a sweet source to draw from. Do so.

6 This is an excellent and inexhaustible well, it should not be covered or doubted.

Great good fortune.

Hexagram 49
Revolution

The Statement

When your day has come, people will believe you. Once a man had sailed around the world, the most eloquent argument for a flat world could not keep people from buying goods from the other side of the globe, or from hearing the truth about how they were transported.

The ancient Chinese idea of the Mandate of Heaven, conferred upon and claimed by each successive ruling dynasty, is, practically speaking, not so very different from the revolutionary notions set forth by the American founding fathers. The mandate is granted to those who are right and is taken away from the tyrannical and ineffective. This is typically accomplished by revolution: new ideas spread and the need for change is proposed, usually rejected out of hand, and a struggle ensues.

For you, the day is fast approaching when the pendulum of acceptance moves to your side of things.

You should do your best not to embody the idea in the old Who song, where it is sung: "Meet the new boss, same as the old boss." Rather, embrace positive change and remember how it felt to be outside looking in.

The Lines

1 You appear to be bound by old circumstances or are just now binding to the new order, but in either interpretation, the time is not yet ripe for action.

2 You may begin to plan for the changes you envision.

3 Let there be at least three rounds of talks before you let yourself be persuaded to action.

The streets of Paris, Moscow and many other cities in upheaval have run very thick with the blood of overzealous revolutionaries, whose timing was just a little off, and whose factions eventually prevailed, without them.

4 Make your move now, and do not be afraid to think on your feet, adapting to meet what will possibly become very rapid, sweeping change.

5 Momentum brings you confidence and enthusiastic converts to your very decisive vision of change.

Go for it.

6 The crowd is fickle and many of those who work the crowd, as Bob Dylan wrote "just want to be on the side that's winning." The true revolutionary has changed, inside and out, but still may have to manage an inevitable mood of backlash. This could come when unrealistic revolutionary expectations are pressed up against the longstanding, deeply entrenched problems, which made revolution necessary in the first place. Be careful.

Having won a revolution, now be still and see what develops around you.

Hexagram 50
The Cauldron

The Statement

Supreme good fortune.

It is easy to see how a Bronze Age cooking pot on three legs came to symbolize the relationship between heaven , the people and the ruler.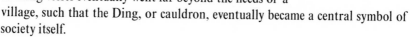

Nothing is more basic to social stability than a full stomach, and competition to decorate and enlarge the cooking vessel eventually went far beyond the needs of a village, such that the Ding, or cauldron, eventually became a central symbol of society itself.

Important jade and gold inscriptions and ultimately, a sacred ceremonial status came to symbolize all the essential attributes of the Way, as the Ding.

The good ruler, himself empty of self-concern, accepted and distributed the bounty of heaven and the people were continuously nourished, both materially and spiritually.

The Lines

1 When a cauldron is overturned, it cannot be used, but it can be cleaned for later use. Here there is an element of intentional or improvisational advantage in an inconvenient situation.

2 Your cauldron is full of good food, and adversaries who are not doing so well, do not even dare to approach you.

3 The handles have come off your cauldron and the food cannot be distributed as it should be, but a blessing rain is coming and difficulties are soon to be overcome.

4 Something is fundamentally wrong with this situation, as if the feet of the cauldron suddenly break, spilling what was to have been a sacred offering, or a feast, and staining you, as well.

Misfortune.

5 Here the cauldron is solid, its handles are golden. All is well.

6 All the best practical and ceremonial appliances of a feast are available to you now. This is a sign of great good fortune, in any of your undertakings.

Hexagram 51
Thunder

The Statement

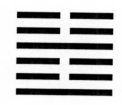

A sonic boom, out of nowhere and shocking our senses is a good measure of concentration and composure.

The ideal here is to be the person whose wisdom and experience remembers this: the fact that we are hearing thunder means, first of all, that whatever danger goes with it is not too close to our person just yet.

The deft surgeon takes a breath but does not drop his scalpel, and the experienced priest spills no sacrificial wine, startling as things may be.

Still, a night of continuous, deafening thunder surely means that shocking changes could be taking place, and self-examination is in order. Be prepared; an unexpected change is probably at hand.

The Lines

1 The shock here is not significant – laughable even – and is followed by good fortune.

2 A shocking loss is temporary. Don't freak out, in a week or so you will get everything back.

3 It may be a good idea to go down to the basement during this storm, or take some other ordinary precaution. Then you will be fine.

4 Lightning and mudslides are coming; scary, but ultimately only a minor disruption for you personally.

5 Sometimes, even in the midst of tornado sirens and general panic, you must attend to your own business, which is, at the moment, more important. Nothing much will be lost.

6 Other times, you can clearly see that a situation is too dangerous to proceed. Take cover, and stay calm.

Others may sustain considerable loss and feel jealous that you came out all right, but you cannot blame yourself for that.

Hexagram 52
Stillness

The Statement

Come to rest, still your back and do not move your body.

Sounds like yoga instruction, doesn't it? It is.

If there is activity around you, pay no attention to it.

You could say that a mountain is nothing but a pile of rocks and dirt, until, that is, you have to climb one or go around it; then you find out differently. A mountain just stands there, but huge effort is required to overcome it in any way.

The power of stillness in a world of continuous change is enormous at the right time, and this is the time to immerse your self in that power.

The Lines

1 Again with the stilling of the toes. Pretty obviously, the idea is to stop whatever is going on before it has gone very far at all. Another possible interpretation could be, though, to be so still that not even a toe is moved.

2 Another good time to be still is when we either have no support from others or cannot make contact with those who should be our support. We will be unhappy about it, but that is better, evidently, than what would happen if we blunder ahead on our own now.

3 You want to move so bad, but are restrained by circumstances, and it is as if your back begins to spasm spontaneously against the strain. There is something heartbreaking about this apparently cruel restraint, but nothing to be done except endure.

4 Recognizing the time of stillness, we come to rest. Good.

5 Stillness is not just for the trunk of the body, we should stop talking as well.

If something must be said, let it be concise.

6 The highest form of stillness is the transcendence of changes in the world, as all our baser desires and internal chatter come to rest, as well. This is good fortune in itself and it brings great fortune to future circumstances, as a matter of course.

Hexagram 53
Easy Does It

The Statement

This is a good phrase for this hexagram, because it does not mean "take it easy", it is all about a gradual, well-considered way of working toward a goal, with planning and effort timed to create the desired results.

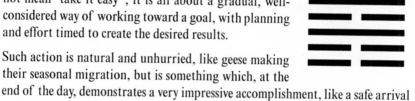

Such action is natural and unhurried, like geese making their seasonal migration, but is something which, at the end of the day, demonstrates a very impressive accomplishment, like a safe arrival at the mating grounds.

The Lines

1 Of course, there are potential dangers on any journey, especially for the inexperienced, and you may be criticized for being too slow. So be it.

2 Here you arrive at a safe destination where you can eat and drink at ease. Good fortune.

3 You may know what you are doing, but conditions have changed on your path. Cover has disappeared or predators lie in waiting. You may lose someone of importance and there is nothing to do but try to fight off your enemy.

4 After unexpected trouble, you may have to improvise to find a decent spot to stop, rest and regroup.

5 This is like geese flying over the last mountain before they reach their destination: it is an exhilarating sight and it is all clear sailing from here. Good Fortune.

6 All necessary travel and important work is completed; you can now concentrate on spiritual matters and enjoy life. Great good fortune.

Hexagram 54
A Backstreet Girl

The Statement

There isn't really a phrase in English to express the non-person status of a secondary wife in ancient China, unless you were to call someone a slave-wife, or something like that.

By arrangement or due to a shotgun-type wedding, the subject here has no independent status or power in the situation, no resources of her own and, like Cinderella, only an interceding miracle is going to create an opportunity for change, but no such hope is offered in the statement here. Nothing furthers at this time.

Nothing, that is, except the ever-present reality of change itself, and to avoid ruin now could set the stage for later gain.

The Lines

1 The lame can walk, and to make the best of a bad situation, it is best to get going.

2 A one-eyed person can see (the limitations of the situation), and you can go it alone if you have to.

3 An old maid, one who has waited either for a better marriage or who was not asked to marry, eventually finds an unsatisfactory union, or, at least, much less than what was hoped for.

4 Here, waiting for a good union does pay off, better late than never.

5 There is a kind of fragility to the relationships in this line, and making a success of it will depend on patience and subtlety. If it can be pulled off despite circumstances that are less than ideal, then good fortune will come near the full moon.

How?

By doing the best you can in every way.

6 To bring an empty basket to a ceremony or feast, to sacrifice a ram from which no blood will flow – it doesn't get any more doom-laden than this in Omenville.

What ought to be, what has been hoped for, simply cannot come to fruition.

Hexagram 55
Abundance

The Statement

Abundance and progress.

Do not worry or regret things past; shine like a crown jewel in the noonday sun.

Shine like the enlightened ruler himself.

The Lines

1 Soul mates, best friends, or a very close teacher-student relationship is indicated, and despite the fact that you are almost too much alike, you should go forward with your plans together, it will be good.

2 Sometimes you must hold your peace, despite the fact that you are right and you know it. If you speak you will invite suspicion, so only say what can be easily shown to be true.

You may suffer an anxiety attack in the face of such weird circumstances, but if you live the truth, rather than trying to talk it, you will be alright.

3 Even in a time of abundance, or in this case maybe because of it, there is a lot going on and not all of it is good. An eclipse is mentioned, but I think that it really indicates a powerful time to test your ability to discern the real from the shadow, in the midst of all this luxury and amid the subtleties of an expanded social agenda that seem always to attend it.

You could meet, completely innocently, with an accident while going about your business.

But, like an eclipse, the bad time will not last long.

4 The usual midday light becomes strange in an eclipse, so that you can see things usually hidden in daylight, like the northern star. It is unsettling, but if you meet with your close friends and advisors, you will be reassured and obtain good fortune.

It may be that while you do not see what is happening here, someone very close to you will see quite clearly, and hence the good auspice.

5 You are surrounded by able, even brilliant, people with whom you will share prosperity and congratulations.

This is the line of the good manager or ruler, who has recognized the right people to befriend and employ in important undertakings.

6 If you have withdrawn from good company and counsel, or decided to hoard all the abundance for yourself, you will be left alone all right, completely alone and lonely.

Hexagram 56
The Traveler

The Statement

There have always been nomads, gypsies, and travelling salesmen of one kind or another, and conditions have made travelers of entire civilizations from time to time.

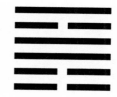

It can be a good thing or not, but with skill and perseverance, travel can bring considerable gain, and a wealth of experience and wisdom as well.

The Lines

1 If you act like you don't know what you are doing, like you don't belong where you are, this is an invitation to being taken advantage of by thieves or highwaymen.

The traveler here is not cautious, not steady or alert enough, and suffers for it.

2 Someone knows the ropes, stops for lodging at the right place and time, puts his valuables in a safe place, and gets his directions straight. He will have a nice stay.

3 You can quickly lose the good will of the locals if you screw up, ignore local etiquette, or do something boneheaded like start a fire in dry, windy country. And the results are then, of course, quite bad.

4 This traveler seems to be doing rather well, getting lodging and safeguarding his tools and valuables, but something is not right. The Oracle is unhappy with this result for some reason.

Maybe things could have gone much better by taking a different course.

Maybe spiritual values have been neglected or perhaps the Oracle simply compassionately shares your own dissatisfaction with a merely acceptable result.

It depends on your situation.

5 A hunter is inevitably a traveler as well, and in this case, is so good at it that it leads to admiration and blessings. You get what you are aiming for and much more.

6 Fate laughs last at someone who finds amusement in another's misfortune. It is as if a callous traveler is guffawing to see a guy sweating, changing his blown tire in the mid-summer heat, only to turn his head and notice his own engine has caught fire.

Hexagram 57
Wind

The Statement

Among the many forces of nature that we take for granted but hardly understand is this pervasive movement of the atmosphere we call *wind*. If you don't think this to be mysterious, check how often the weatherman has to revise his predictions, even with all the technology at our modern command.

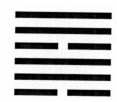

The situation calls for incremental progress and a gentle, yielding but steady motion toward our goals. Do not overlook the importance of small or mild influences.

I would say that the life and work of Mahatma Gandhi is a good example of the ideal expressed in this hexagram.

He overcame great powers with mildness, prayer, and fasting; at last even his adversaries praised his virtue.

The Lines

1 Advancing and retreating are both useful to a warrior, at the appropriate times. A dance of timing and acceptance is indicated.

2 Something is going on that will require all your spiritual resources to be employed.

Prayer, meditation, intentional dreaming, whatever you are comfortable with, use it.

It may be a very subtle or confusing task, but you can achieve good fortune once you have done all you can to influence the situation in a positive way.

3 A dark, negative energy, like an endless ill wind or some low-key but relentless stress, has penetrated this situation. Misfortune.

4 This is not exactly a windfall, because it is your own considerable efforts that meet with success, perhaps three times, and disappointment disappears.

5 This is a windfall, but who can say where the wind begins? You must contemplate the situation for some time, perhaps three days, and then you will be in the right place at the right time to act, and you'll enjoy considerable good fortune, perhaps for another three days.

6 Here an ill wind blows away everything you have worked for in this circumstance. This is serious misfortune.

Hexagram 58
Sharing

The Statement

As two conjoined lakes share the same water and wildlife, people in relationship with one another can share all the delights of life in celebration of progress, wealth and wisdom.

The Lines

1 Sharing mutual satisfaction, there is good fortune.

2 When your own joy is shared sincerely, it attracts more good fortune and any regrets are easily overcome.

3 This is a mixed bag: there is some pleasure and some pain to be shared now or on the way soon. Or it is possible that expecting some kind of enjoyment which has not yet fully manifested itself is the only (and quite likely illusory) misfortune that will be experienced.

4 There is no use sharing a lot of nervous talk regarding some hoped for future enjoyment.

Avoid it, and trust that a good outcome is likely.

5 Relationships that are based only on pleasure fall apart quickly when no gratification is in evidence. There is danger in such sharing, and it could be a rude awakening.

6 Sometimes we get caught up in the pursuit of enjoyment or are led in that direction by others.

It could be a good thing or a bad thing, but it is certainly a seductive form of sharing, so discrimination and good character, obviously, will be most important.

Hexagram 59
Distribution

The Statement

After Sitting Bull finally surrendered to save what was left of his people from starvation, he did a brief stint with Buffalo Bill's Wild West Show, among other things.

He traveled all around the U.S., went to Europe and upon returning to see the newly industrialized New York City, he was asked to give his impression of all the modern marvels he had seen. He said "The white man knows how to make everything, but not how to distribute."

He was, of course, not talking about the ability to move things from place to place to those who could afford them. He was talking about what, to the chief's mind, must have been an incomprehensible imbalance between the great concentration of goods in a few places, while people starved to death in other places, even nearby.

In this hexagram, the distribution of all good things, material and spiritual, is encouraged to ensure success and perseverance is stressed.

You may be called upon to travel. You are reminded not to neglect your spiritual responsibilities. Authorities could act to spread the wealth.

The Lines

1 The strength of a horse, or some other reliable vehicle, is made available to save the day and ensure good fortune.

2 While things around you may be falling apart, or in disarray, your own place of spiritual power is safe and that is where you need to be, to avoid regret.

3 Sometimes the need for distribution and help is so urgent that you must completely forget your own self-interest, in favor of the plight of others. This is noble and entirely blameless.

4 There are subtle cross-purposes at work here, and there is no fault in letting the voicemails pile up until you can sort out what people are up to.

Then you will know who is on the same page that you are on, and reassemble the true friends and allies, after some soul searching.

5 Someone in a position of responsibility or authority (maybe you) is really sweating it right now, and issues orders and fires off memos with unusual urgency. Fortunately he has read the situation clearly and makes the necessary distributions in time to avoid real trouble.

6 The situation is serious and you may have to take radical action or leave the scene to preserve yourself. Someone may even be contemplating violence. Do not sacrifice more than this is worth. You must decide.

Hexagram 60
Control and Self Control

The Statement

As a culture we Americans are all about liberty and individual freedom to do what we want, and we tend to take a dim view of limitation, restraint or regulation, as a matter of course.

But if what you want to do is accomplish something, you immediately become aware of the need to learn the discipline and limitations involved in your undertaking.

It doesn't matter whether it is building a house, doing brain surgery, or playing stunning rock guitar solos – a lot of self-control must be learned before the freedom to act is more than a useless fantasy.

On the other hand, being made to sit and play scales, when you really wanted to be outside playing baseball, has not produced a lot of great musicians, and having someone constantly on your case to study harder so you can get into medical school and be somebody, has probably not produced the majority of top brain surgeons, either.

Harsh control tends to fail; self-control that seeks the freedom of self-assured action, does a lot better.

The Lines

1 This is a time for simple self-control. Stay home or if that is not possible, take the most conservative course of action available to you.

2 This is a time when staying at home is a mistake and there are, evidently, things that need to be done, so get out there and do them.

3 If you have failed to control yourself or practice sufficient discipline even though all necessary opportunities were available, you are going to regret it, even though this is a situation where nobody else will blame you… or maybe you're the only one who knows.

4 A person who learns to enjoy self-control, or feels comfortable being told what to do by an authority figure, can make progress in this situation.

5 The person who is willing to go a little further with self-discipline, like the athlete who stays the extra hours at the gym to become his very best, can win honor and achieve good fortune now.

6 Harsh and bitter control, endless work or study, punishing physical workouts or just the stress of having to tolerate a dictatorial control freak, is a misfortune in itself, and gets bad results.

In time this trouble will pass.

Hexagram 61
Free At Heart

The Statement

Enlightened confidence, intelligence, peace of mind, heartfelt sincerity – these will move even the lowest and most stubborn creatures and bring good fortune.

One who is free at heart can undertake the most difficult things successfully.

He looks at you and sees a person, he glances in the mirror and only sees another person, yet everywhere he looks, he sees the Divine.

The Lines

1 He will know good fortune when others are ill at ease.

Having found himself, he is at ease with good fortune.

If he seeks another, he will witness misfortune.

(This is a paradox of enlightenment; for the man of understanding there is really only wellbeing. Still, there are always others, it seems, gathered around even one who has withdrawn from the world, and he is sure to compassionately notice their misfortunes.)

2 Wine drinking is older even than the Book of Changes.

Here it is as if one hears a crane calling and at peace, which reminds us to call out to a friend and offer some of our excellent wine, a sign of both material wellbeing and spiritual friendship.

3 An enemy force is encountered but is no match for us. Some halt, some weep, some beat a drum, but all panic in the face of such confidence.

4 Things are not completed, but like the moon nearly full, we can rest assured that completion is close upon us. Someone or something may go astray, but can be replaced.

5 This is a line of masterful and confident union, without error.

6 There is a great deal of difference between an experience of being enlightened and having actually become an enlightened being.

It is on the order of the difference between having played a great piano recital, and actually being Mozart, for example.

Here there have been good signs and good progress, but in the end considerable trouble comes because of overestimation, overconfidence, overambitious expectations or having otherwise turned, somehow, from the way.

Hexagram 62
Smallness

The Statement

If you are asking about a little detail in some small matter, the news is good. If you are asking about how things look for a major undertaking, not so.

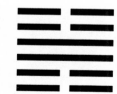

Keep your feet on the ground, and exercise more than usual caution. Then small things can lead to good results.

The Lines

1 As birds must flee from famine, you must change your relationship to the matter in question.

2 You may have greater spiritual and material ambitions than the times will support, but you will get some of what you seek, and that is enough for now.

3 Take every possible precaution against very real possible danger and/or injury.

Do not pursue big plans such as, in the traditional metaphor, crossing a great waterway.

4 I don't imagine that the words "absolutely refrain" have changed much over time.

It is very precise advice and if taken to heart, should save you from serious trouble.

Do not act.

5 There seems to be some ancient coded message in this line. I take it to mean that, while some good things are very near, like a good rain to break a cycle of drought and famine, they are not here yet and this causes anxiety.

So you must take what you can get to help you endure the time, and it may not be all that easy. A hunter's quickness and stamina are called for here.

But, like Gloria Gaynor, you will survive.

6 There is a potential disaster here, either from trying to soar too high too fast or from missing the one element in the situation, no doubt something small, that can save you (perhaps a meeting with someone you might be inclined to see as unimportant).

Try to avoid such a blunder, because it is all on you.

Hexagram 63
Completion

The Statement

The Book of Changes does not close with the time of Completion, as if it were a Hollywood movie. It closes with the next Hexagram, Unfinished Business, because it is about real life.

Something is indeed successfully completed here, like a rough river crossing, but the gain is small and you are advised to continue with all the wisdom and perseverance demonstrated in the previous lessons of the Oracle.

Things look good now, but could still take a turn toward disorder, and the inevitability of change includes even an awareness of possible calamity. So consideration of the unforeseen needs to be perpetual – such is real life.

The Lines

1 While crossing this metaphorical river your vehicle (possibly you) may have sustained some minor damage. So what? You made it.

2 Something ornamental or not terribly significant is lost in transit, don't chase after it.

You will get it back, maybe in a week.

3 After a long struggle with the forces against you, you succeed. Do not employ anything less than the best qualified people you can find now, as such people will be worse than useless in major undertakings.

4 Here is someone who is still trying to get across; his boat leaks but he has rags to fill the holes.

Stay on guard until the crossing is finished; anything is still possible.

5 Now we see someone (perhaps in the east) making extravagant offerings to please the Divine, but lacking depth of sincerity, while another man (in the west) has little to offer in material terms, but his extraordinary devotion makes his gifts more acceptable. This, of course, brings him happiness.

6 Just when the crossing is nearly complete, you lose your footing or the river surges, and find yourself in over your head. The results cannot be good.

Hexagram 64

Unfinished Business

The Statement

We are back at the beginning of the circle of the Tao, here in the final Hexagram, perhaps trying our first crossing of a big river. We have no choice but to continue, and we may succeed, like a clever young fox whose instincts take him across, only getting his tail a little wet.

But this is only one possibility in a situation with serious, inherent dangers.

So, as one who has perused the Book of Changes, did you think you could become careless or take it easy before the crossing is completed?

Of course not.

Stay balanced and alert, you will probably be fine.

The Lines

1 The fox's tail has grown heavy with water. At the least this will slow his crossing, to his sorrow.

2 A man's got to do what a man's got to do, and in this case he's got to drag his heavy cart across the river. This will be arduous but successful.

3 Just part of the way into a river crossing for military or other adversarial purposes, you realize that your location is no good for the foray you wish to make. You improvise and land further down the river, out of harm's way.

4 It may take some time and you may have to be aggressive, but fortune is with you and the rewards will be great, as your cause is just.

5 All the noble attributes are shown in the subject of this line; his undertakings, therefore, are blessed with good fortune.

6 Rice wine was first made a few millennia before even the appearance of the *I Ching*.

From the beginning it was used socially, medicinally and as a sacramental offering.

Wine would have been imbibed to celebrate a successful crossing of a great river, a recurring topic in the Oracle.

But wine was also, no doubt, even from the beginning, sometimes used to excess.

Here a warning against such excess is given, exactly as if it carried the same danger as being submerged during a river crossing. Something could swamp you, if you are not careful.

But luck comes to the man of solid determination. He takes a vow, and continues on to even greater good fortune.

Afterword

So, having finished the main body of *The Street Corner Ching* some time ago, this morning I asked it if I should write a brief afterword to the text, to sum up the experience.

I received the sixth line of Hexagram 53. That's essentially a yes with the further indication that the task could be somewhat troublesome (Hexagram 39).

The trouble is that this work is many things.

It is, of course, an interpretation of the venerable Chinese oracles. But it also is a process. It is interactive. It is a relationship. It can be as real and tangible as any relationship in the world, and yet, it must be admitted, the process appears for all the world to take place entirely within the mind.

But where exactly is the dimensional limit of mind? Such a limit may be presumed, but in reality it can never be found. The moment such a limit is conceived, the mind has already been there.

So one main purpose of this book is to provide our minds access to the dimension of time we call the future. We have our desires and hopes and we have our doubts and anxieties about all kinds of circumstances. We have the personality we currently seem to be and perhaps, the character we would hope to become, in mind. And all of this, inevitably, is reflected back to us in this interaction.

We come with questions, and the answers we get, as often as not, will require some serious contemplation to be understood. Our subjective response will be just as important to the value of a reading as the actual text of the answer.

It is best to come with an open mind and heart.

But many people simply cannot believe in the veracity of this work. They would perhaps argue that it is unscientific. Others will believe that there is something to it, but will have trouble finding useful interpretations. So a serious interaction with the Oracle, obviously, is not for everyone.

But doubt, ultimately, is merely the yin to belief's yang. What you doubt now, you may at some point find to be more acceptable. If you can suspend your disbelief for a few moments, you may be surprised and delighted with what you find. That is my hope.

If you already share my enthusiasm for this work, then my hope is to have provided a version that will perhaps be a little more resonant to your ear and a little easier to understand than some of the other editions of the *I Ching*.

I was reading a little bit about quantum discoveries in physics yesterday, and the inherent fluidity and multidimensionality of it all reminded me of the yin/yang emblem of the Tao.

There was a previously held view fundamental to physics, for example, that a particle can never be a wave, but new technology seems to reveal conditions where particles do, in fact, shape-shift into waves, and then sometimes pop into utter non-existence (or some unknown dimension). Other recent discoveries indicate that the largest part of the universe now seems to be made of stuff called dark matter and dark energy, and is essentially unobservable by humans at the present time. Science does, therefore, appear to be yielding a pretty mystical view of even the physical universe, the more we learn.

So where exactly could these wonders fit into the physics of a universe with any meaningful constants?

Only a view that allows for a dance of polarities of infinite scale and dimensionality can account for these matters.

Things could be yin now and yang later, and at some point a thing may seem to be two things and then no thing at all. It is all apparently about timing but the time is, somehow, always: now. Our own humble lives, in my view, are ultimately also of just such a paradoxical nature. Perhaps this is why the Oracle rarely indicates a simple yes or no when consulted.

Fortunately, however, the vast majority of our concerns will be far simpler than the mysteries of quantum physics, and our questions, in general, will be far easier to address.

The Book of Changes knows all about it.

The answers we seek and the lessons we learn yield, in time, to more sophisticated occasions of questioning because we are creatures of continuous growth and change ourselves.

But, in the process, we have passed through circumstances, extraordinary or mundane, with a new or renewed sense that there really is a spiritual dimension to our human lives.

We throw the coins, look up our answer, and see that this work has much to offer and teach us.

LaVergne, TN USA
14 April 2010
179293LV00002B/94/P